LEARNING TO FLY

RADIO CONTROL
MODEL AIRPLANES

RC PERFORMANCE SERIES No. 5

BY JOHN CARROLL

Editor: Burr Angle
Art Director: Lawrence Luser
Editorial Assistant: Marcia Stern
Art and Layout: Wells S. Marshall, III

KALMBACH BOOKS

First printing, 1985. Second printing, 1986. Third printing, 1987. Fourth printing, 1989. Fifth printing, 1990.

If you're thinking of becoming a radio control model aviator, a visit to an RC club flying field will whet your interest.

1. Getting started

Several friends of mine who pilot commercial airliners habitually park their DC-9s and 737s at Dulles Airport and head straight for the radio control field. There's something magic about our little airplanes that even full-size aviation doesn't provide. And the fascination doesn't stop with professional pilots. On weekends our Northern Virginia Radio Control (NVRC) club field near Arcola, Virginia, may have 40 people of all descriptions and 100 planes, at least two of which are aloft even during slack times. There are tiny models with wingspans of three feet and monsters that stand nearly waist high. There are multiengine planes, powered gliders, biplanes, military planes, civilian planes, and even a space shuttle that rides to altitude on the back of a "sort-of-747" and flies back to earth under the control of its own pilot. Everywhere there are trainers and sport planes.

Occasionally we have fun flies, which is about as close as most of us come to competition. On those days, we risk our planes flying under three-foot-high ribbons, or trying to cram too many take-offs and landings into two minutes, or at the winter "Snow Fly" contest, flying planes with ill-fitting skis.

The rest of the time we're not a competitive lot. Mostly we just do whatever comes naturally, which is sometimes flying, sometimes talking, and sometimes sitting under a tent on a hot sum-

mer day relaxing and watching others fly.

For us and most other RC pilots, the hobby centers around a club. Newcomers learn under the tutelage of old-timers, and everyone learns from others' successes and failures. Each personality shows up in the kinds of planes flown and the way they are handled in the air and on the ground. There are strict safety rules, but no regimentation, and within reason, everyone does what he feels like doing. It's a club. It's a place to go when you need to forget the job or when you want to show off a little or you'd just like an excuse to be outdoors.

There's more to RC than lazing around the field, of course. Building an RC model requires hard work and several hundred dollars. Learning to fly requires discipline and a tolerance for frustration. Almost anybody can do both, but it takes work. Some people get into the hobby with the idea that it's going to be a snap — I did. My original plan was to build a plane, learn to fly it in an afternoon, and go on to other things. It didn't happen that way, and despite a lot of hard work, it was months before I could confidently take off and land. Years later, I'm still learning new flying techniques.

Even an RC trainer is more difficult to fly than a full-size Cub or Cessna. In some respects, I've been told, it's tougher to handle than an F-16 fighter. But you'll master the basics on your trainer, and when you do, there will be something else to learn. If you can fly a trainer, you'll want to try a low-wing sport plane. If you can fly that, you'll want a scale model. You'll worry about design and equipment and radio performance and getting the new plane done on time. Sometimes it will be as tough as your job, but if you're like the rest of us, you'll enjoy even the problems.

This book is primarily about learning to fly radio control model airplanes but because you need a good plane and a suitable engine to fly well it is also to

3

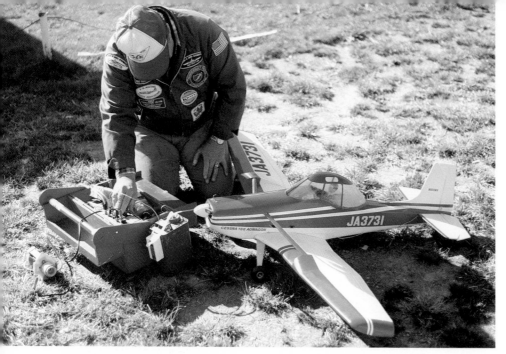

The Northern Virginia Radio Control club has nearly 300 members — on a summer day it sometimes seems that all of us are at the field tinkering with engines, practicing simple and advanced aerobatics, or just talking with each other.

some extent about building and buying. In the chapters that follow, I will tell you how to find a club, choose a kit, avoid major building mistakes, and select a flight instructor. Mostly, though, the subject will be flying: how to take off, fly the traffic pattern, and land; how to handle the plane in windy weather; and how to fly simple and advanced aerobatic maneuvers.

The book won't make you a competent pilot any more than a book on driving will make a beginner safe in Manhattan's rush hour traffic, but it is based on tested methods and will help you avoid the worst mistakes; it will more

than pay for itself in crashes avoided.

How to use this book. If you haven't started in RC flying yet, read the whole book before you do. If you already own equipment, or even if you have a plane almost ready to go, stop what you're doing and read; it will save you more time than it takes. As you progress through each stage of learning to fly, carefully re-read the part that pertains to what you're about to do.

Finally, especially with the flying chapters, after you've gotten your feet wet, come back to the book again. You'll find things you didn't notice the first time, or even the second, that are

suddenly meaningful. For instance, the part on maintaining altitude in a turn will make more sense after you've turned once or twice. In fact, it's a good idea to bring the book to the flying field so that after each flight, while events are still fresh in your mind, you can check what you and your plane did against what should have happened and make corrections during the next flight.

If you are like most of us, it will take you a season or two to make the transition from novice to proficient pilot. It's not easy, but for most of us, it's not easy to quit, either.

Now visit the local hobby shop and talk to the people behind the counter, remembering that they are in business to sell and that often they are not RC modelers. Look at the models, radio equipment, and engines on display and get a rough idea of the costs involved. If you buy anything at all on the first visit, let it be a model magazine, not RC equipment.

Finding an RC club. After you've looked at the shop's wares, ask where people in your area fly, whether there is a local club, and if so, how to contact it. You're going to need a flying field and lots of help, and a club is usually the best source of both.

If for some reason the hobby shop people don't know how to reach the club (oddly enough, they sometimes don't) contact the Academy of Model Aeronautics (AMA) and ask for a list of clubs in your area. The AMA's address is 1810 Samuel Morse Drive, Reston, VA 22090; the phone number is (703) 435-0750.

If you join a club, you will almost certainly be required to join the AMA and if you can't find a club, you'd be well advised to join the AMA on your own because with your membership comes up to two million dollars of liability insurance.

Once you've found the club (if there is none nearby and you can't find a competent RC pilot to help you, see Chapter 11 on teaching yourself how to fly) make an appointment to visit the field. Plan to spend some time there, and don't hesitate to introduce yourself to members and say you're thinking of getting into the hobby. The flying field is as much a social hall as a model airport; the veterans are proud of their equipment and knowledge and most are glad to help a newcomer. Ask about everything and then just listen to the old-timers. Most RC pilots will talk endlessly about the hobby and their planes. They may not be world experts, but most know more about the hobby than the beginner, so they are worth listening to.

If you hang around long enough, you'll get almost everybody's opinion. You'll also get a look at planes in flight and a feel for the kinds of engines and

We are inveterate experimenters, as shown by Luther Hux's scale model space shuttle, which rides to altitude aboard Bill Hershberger's "sort-of-747." After release, Luther guides the shuttle back to the runway for a hot landing.

radio equipment favored by club members. Even more important, you'll see who flies well and who doesn't.

Choosing an instructor. Selecting an instructor is your first important decision in learning to fly, and unlike full-size aviation, where flight instructors are certified according to a uniform set of requirements, there is no guarantee in many clubs that your instructor will be competent. Worse, you probably will have several instructors during your apprenticeship, and if one of them is a jerk, he can cost you an airplane. Make sure that guy can fly his plane. Make sure that guy can fly his own plane before you let him touch yours. I know that last comment should go without saying, but the fact is that more than a few beginners get burned by an unqualified and overeager pilot

(Right) Even in winter the field is busy. Here models line up awaiting their turns to take off. (Above) When snow arrives, we fit homemade skis to the planes.

Trainer cords take most of the danger out of learning to fly RC. The transmitters are of the same make and model.

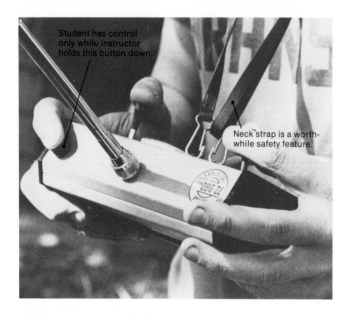

Student has control only while instructor holds this button down.

Neck strap is a worth-while safety feature.

With a trainer cord, the instructor can take control instantly by simply lifting his right index finger off the button.

Wind sock

Frequency pins

Impounded transmitters

The control tower at the NVRC field sports a wind sock to tell pilots which way to take off and land. It also serves as a transmitter impound stand. Transmitters are placed on the stand when not in use and may be removed only when the pilot has possession of the appropriate frequency pin. The pin must be clipped to his transmitter before it can be turned on.

who can't wait to risk somebody else's plane. If you spend time at the field before your own plane is ready, you can identify and avoid those guys.

There are other things to learn at the field; for example, you can find out which of the good pilots, if any, use transmitters designed for trainer cords (also called buddy cords). When a student's transmitter is hooked to an instructor's by a trainer cord, the instructor can take control at any time by simply lifting his finger off a button. This is much easier on airplanes than

the more common method of passing the transmitter back to your instructor when you get into trouble. Unfortunately, most of the newer transmitters do not have the trainer cord feature, and those that do can normally be hooked up only to others of the same brand and model. Still, it's worth checking. You may find an instructor whose equipment is suitable for use with a cord. If you do, buy a system compatible with his.

Another reason you should spend as much time as possible at the flying

field is to learn the formal and informal rules — where to fly and where not to fly, for example, and such bits of etiquette as not running your engine where it will spit grease on someone else's car, and how to deal with the traffic pattern on landings and take-offs. Most important, learn the procedures that ensure you don't fly on someone else's frequency. While you're sopping up this education from the club veterans, you can begin to acquire the equipment you'll need to become one of them.

If you must learn to fly without an instructor, try one of the small foam models sold by Cox Hobbies. They look much like the Ranger shown here. The Ranger was at least as good as the Cox planes, but is no longer on the market.

2. Choosing equipment

My friend Larry Parfitt, a retired fighter pilot who works part-time in a hobby shop, has asked me to tell beginners to keep it simple when buying equipment. He said this after telling me about a guy who came into the shop, bought some fancy radio gear, said he was going to put it in his Pitts Special, and then admitted he'd never flown RC. Larry told him to set the Pitts aside because it was a biplane, because it was too responsive, because it was a tail-dragger (no nosewheel), and because it was too elaborate and expensive to learn on.

Unfortunately, many beginners end up in the position of Larry's customer.

Someone gives or sells them a finished model or a kit that's too much to handle, or perhaps they just don't consult anyone before buying a kit that's too hot or too difficult to build. Larry has a special message for former fighter jocks like himself — no matter how many combat missions you've flown, you can't simply pick up a transmitter and fly a hot RC model. That message also applies to non-pilots, of course. Regardless of your background, start with a docile airplane and an experienced instructor. If you already own a hot plane, set it aside, sell it, or convert it to a trainer.

Understand that the choice is not be-

tween taking a high risk and playing it safe. If you take a high-performance RC plane up by yourself, it has as much chance of surviving as if you threw it into a furnace. Even with the best of instruction, you need a docile plane. If you own a biplane, don't put it into the air. If you have a tail-dragger, don't put it up. If it has a low wing, leave it on the shelf. If it's expensive or takes a long time to build, set it aside for the time being. The same advice holds for almost all scale models and all giant scale models powered by chain saw engines.

What to look for in a trainer. The list of things not to start with is endless, so rather than tell you what not to buy, I'll list the features to look for in a trainer:

1. It should be a high-wing airplane because high wings give more stable flying characteristics.

2. It should be light and have a big wing. Most kit box labels state the approximate flying weight and wing area. To find out if the ratio is right, divide the flying weight in ounces by the wing area in square feet to determine the wing loading. If the plane is a good trainer, your answer will be no more than 17 ounces per square foot. The heavier the wing loading the faster the plane will have to move to stay airborne and the less time you'll have to correct mistakes. Further, a heavily loaded wing tends to stall more violently than a lightly loaded one.

3. It should have a tricycle landing gear because a plane with a nosewheel is easier to take off and land than a tail-dragger.

4. It should be relatively inexpensive and easy to build. You are going to beat it up and repair it at least a couple of times, so save the fancy planes until later when you'll only have to build them once.

5. The kit should contain clear and complete assembly instructions. Fortunately, most popular trainers come with excellent instruction booklets and detailed, full-size plans, but check before you buy to make sure yours isn't the exception. A couple of sketches and a page of hints won't do.

6. The model should be powered by a medium-size engine. Ideally, you'll start with a trainer powered by a .40 to .60 engine. (The numbers refer to the engine's cylinder displacement in hundredths of cubic inches — we ignore the decimal point when talking about these engines, so that a .40 is a "forty" and a .60 is a "sixty.") Considerations of cost and space may dictate something smaller, but don't go below a .19 for your first plane.

Many experienced RC pilots insist that big models fly more smoothly. I haven't noticed that to be the case (though they do handle better on bumpy runways), but larger planes are cer-

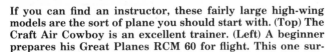

If you can find an instructor, these fairly large high-wing models are the sort of plane you should start with. (Top) The Craft Air Cowboy is an excellent trainer. (Left) A beginner prepares his Great Planes RCM 60 for flight. This one survived several minor accidents before its owner soloed; he is now an accomplished RC pilot. (Right) Probably more people have learned to fly RC on the Goldberg Falcon 56 than any other model; it remains an excellent choice.

tainly easier to fly because they are easier to see. They are also easier to build because there is more room inside for the engine and radio equipment. This extra room also lets you use more foam rubber padding around electronic equipment that can be damaged by vibration.

On the other hand, big planes cost more to build and operate than small ones, take up more space in the house and car, and really big models require sophisticated building techniques.

As in the past, most beginners still start with conventional balsa kits, but almost-ready-to-fly (ARF) models are also worth considering. There have been some good-flying plastic foam ARFs on the market for years, but these have been small airplanes, usually ugly, and not durable. More recently ARFs with wooden skeletons much like those in conventional kits have appeared. They are pretty and the ones I've tested have flown well. Unfortunately, I don't consider any to be basic trainers, but at least one, the Hobby

Shack EZ Super Box Fly-20, can be modified into a trainer that is the equal of any conventional kit on the market. More about the modifications in Chapter 4.

Standard trainers include the Goldberg Eagle, Eaglet, and Falcon; the Sig Kadet; and the RCM 40 and 60. All are excellent, stable airplanes. Take your pick, though I'd go with the slower, flat-bottom airfoils (as on the Eagle, Eaglet, and Kadet) in a first plane because they give the beginner an extra fraction of a second to correct a mistake.

Good trainers. In preparing to write this book, I built three trainers — the Goldberg Eaglet because it is extremely popular and flies well, the EZ Super Box Fly-20 because it is an ARF, and the Goldberg Ranger 42 because it is close to ideal if you have to teach yourself to fly. More about the Ranger in Chapter 11. Here I'll compare the Eaglet and Box Fly, both of which can be built into fine trainers.

The Eaglet is a fairly typical trainer. The kit costs about half as much as a

Box Fly although you must purchase such extras as glue, wheels, covering material, fuel tank, and spinner separately, so the total cost of the completed models is about the same. It took me 40 hours to get the Eaglet into the air; the Box Fly, even with modifications, required less than 20 hours.

The Eaglet flies beautifully, but its aerobatic ability is limited. It can fly inverted, but just barely, and will not do many standard maneuvers. The modified Box Fly will fly inverted as cleanly as it flies upright and will breeze its way through any AMA pattern maneuver you are good enough to fly.

If you were looking for a sport plane, I would recommend the modified Box Fly over the Eaglet — but you aren't. It will be months, and probably a couple of planes, before you fly well enough to push the Eaglet to its limits. So for now, one is as good as the other, and you can choose on the basis of aesthetics and whether you enjoy building for its own sake. If you hate to build, get

(Left) The almost-ready-to-fly EZ Super Box Fly-20 is a great sport plane as it comes from the box. (Right) However, since it's a little too hot for the beginner, I modified the plane by adding to the wing and tail (dark areas), which has the effect of reducing the loading on these surfaces. The result is a very gentle trainer. Chapter 4 tells how to make the changes.

the Box Fly. If you enjoy building, buy the Eaglet or some other conventionally built trainer.

If you choose the Box Fly don't fly it before making the modifications described in Chapter 4. It's a great sport plane as is, but a shade too hot for a basic trainer.

By now you should have a good idea of the kind of plane to buy if you're starting from scratch, but what if you already own a plane that's "almost a trainer"? Let's assume that you are going to have an instructor and that this plane you built or inherited is just a little too hot. You may be able to put "training wheels" on a high-wing plane with a tricycle landing gear by increasing the wing and horizontal stabilizer area, Chapter 4, but there are limits and in some cases your best bet is to sell the plane or set it aside.

So far I've assumed you'll have an instructor, but some of you will have to teach yourselves. I did this and so can you, though it's more difficult. For those who must go that route, I suggest a different kind of airplane. It won't fly

as well as a four-channel trainer, but it is cheap and slow and requires that you deal with only two controls at a time. More important, if you crash it, chances are a little quick-setting epoxy and a few toothpicks will patch it up well enough to fly again in half an hour.

The plane I used to teach myself, and one of only two I recommend, is the Cox Centurion. It comes with an .049 (pronounced "oh-forty-nine") engine already installed and can be flown 30 minutes after you open the box. It responds sluggishly to control inputs, has to be hand launched, and gives only one engine speed — wide open — but is fairly stable and nearly indestructible.

The other plane in this category is the Goldberg Ranger 42, which comes without an engine. I'll discuss both planes in Chapter 11.

Choosing an engine. There are many kinds of engines on the market — two-cycle and four-cycle, diesel, spark-ignition, glow-ignition, and even a Wankel, not to mention electric motors. At most flying fields two-cycle glow-ignition engines predominate, but four-cycles are

becoming popular and you may want to use one, especially if noise is a consideration. Four-cycle engines have a far quieter, less irritating sound, somewhat like the sound of a full-size lightplane. They also cost more and have a lower power-to-weight ratio.

Somewhere on the side of your plane's kit box or in the instructions, you will find the manufacturer's recommended engine sizes, something like ".19 to .45" or ".09 to .25." Unfortunately, it ain't necessarily so, especially if you fly from a grass field. One of the mysteries of RC modeling is why manufacturers' recommendations on engine size are often useless. Worse, not all engines of a given size produce equal power, so let's get those two problems sorted out before going further.

First, the question of power and engine size. The biggest differences among two-cycle glow engines come about because some have standard porting and some are Schnuerle-ported (pronounced "shnure-lee"). Schnuerle-ported engines have one or more additional inlet ports and other special features for increased

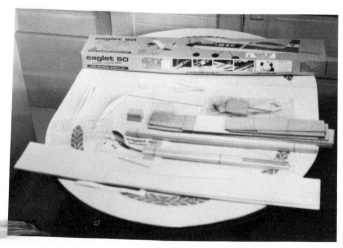

(Left) The Goldberg Eaglet 50 starts out as a woodpile; the kit is well engineered and comes with full-size plans and an illustrated assembly booklet — you could never go wrong with a Goldberg design. (Right) Most almost-ready-to-fly models have polystyrene foam plastic fuselages — I much prefer the Box Fly's lighter, built-up wooden fuselage.

The models looked like this after four hours of work. (Above) The Eaglet's framework is simple, strong, and lightweight. (Right) The Box Fly will be ready to fly in another ten hours.

power — a .25 Schnuerle may be equivalent to a standard .30 or even a .35. Schnuerles are more expensive than standard engines; both types work well, but choose a Schnuerle if there's any question about whether you'll have enough power.

Typical two-cycle glow-ignition RC engines. Top to bottom: Supertigre .60, Enya .35, Supertigre .11, and Cox .049. Each is equipped with a muffler.

Now for the recommendation on the side of the kit box. If a manufacturer says his plane flies well on both an .09 and a .25, be suspicious. The statement may mean that on a smooth concrete runway an .09 will actually get the plane into the air (where it will fly sluggishly), but the plane will require a .25 to take off from a rough grass field. Whenever you see such a wide range of engine sizes, choose the largest. I have yet to see a case where any recommended engine was too powerful.

The Eaglet affair. To illustrate the problem, let me recount the "Eaglet affair" that took place at our flying field one summer. That season there must have been 20 new Eaglets in the club. Many were powered by standard .15 engines and on our grass field they barely managed to take off into a stiff head wind on cold days. When the weather turned hot and humid, the wind died, and engines produced less

power and wings less lift, the .15-powered Eaglets crawled the length of the runway without raising a wheel.

We hand launched them and they reluctantly stayed up but gained altitude slowly. As a result, when a beginner made a mistake and the plane dropped 100 feet, it took forever to recover the lost altitude.

The .15-powered Eaglets were disasters at our field, yet the Eaglet is one of the best small trainers you can buy. The problem is that the manufacturer recommends engine sizes as low as .09, not nearly enough for a grass field, and not enough even in the air, as far as I'm concerned. My own Eaglet, powered by a Schnuerle-ported Fox .19, performed beautifully all summer, as did others with .19 to .25 engines.

One school of thought, apparently left from the early days of RC when many planes didn't have throttle control, insists a beginner should steer

After 40 hours of work, the Eaglet looked like this and flew beautifully.

clear of big engines. Perhaps this is why manufacturers often recommend engines that are too small.

The fact is that with current four-channel radio systems, the danger more often comes from too little power than from too much. With the larger engine, your chances of stalling on takeoff are much less. You need a shorter takeoff run, so your chances of steering errors are less also, which reduces the likelihood of running into a tree or another flier. If you stall, you can recover with less loss of altitude, and if you get too low, you can climb back to a safe height faster — an especially helpful trait on an overshot landing with trees looming ahead. My advice, then, is to choose the largest recommended engine, and to be safe, make it a Schnuerle.

If you decide to use a four-cycle engine, multiply the largest recommended two-cycle displacement by 1.5. For example, if the kit manufacturer says to use a .19 to .25 multiply .25 by 1.5 to get .375; then round up and choose a .40 four-cycle.

If you're still not sure what size engine to use, there are two other ways to find out. The best way is to go to the field and find someone with a plane like yours. What size engine does he use for good performance? If you can't find someone with the same plane, estimate the required engine size by multiplying the weight of your airplane in pounds by .07. For example, if the finished plane will weigh 5 pounds, the engine displacement will be 5 times .07, or .35 cubic inch, and if you install a .35 or .40 engine, you'll be all right. If you use a four-cycle, don't forget to multiply your answer by 1.5. In this case, you would multiply .35 by 1.5 to get .525. There are no .525s on the market, so take the next size up — .60. (These calculations give usable answers for lightly loaded trainers, but don't apply to other kinds of planes, especially scale models.)

As for the brand of engine to use, see what the people around you are flying and try one of the brands that seems to work well. I've owned Fox, Supertigre, O.S., and several other brands and haven't had a bad one yet. There are a few cautions, though. Keep it simple. You don't need a carburetor fuel pump or a tuned pipe. Both have their uses, but not on trainers.

Finally, if you buy a two-cycle engine, check to see if the glow plug has an idle bar. If it doesn't, throw the plug away or give it to someone you don't like. Replace it with a plug that has an idle bar.

Having said you need an idle bar, let me now reverse myself and admit that if your engine is a four-cycle, you don't need one; four-cycles seem to idle just fine on plugs without the bar.

Propellers. The literature that comes with your engine will tell what size

The shiny object running alongside the fuselage is a tuned pipe for increased engine power. Stay away from tuned pipes until you've mastered the basics.

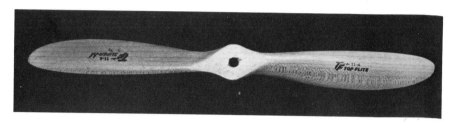

The wooden propeller combines efficient operation with safety and good looks.

(Above) If your two-cycle engine comes with a glow plug like this without an idle bar, replace it. (Right) The bar is a piece of metal on the bottom of the plug.

prop to use, but not what kind, and there are three types in common use. Plain nylon props are the least popular and I don't recommend them, if only because at high speed the blade tips deform until they are half an inch or so ahead of the propeller hub; this must cause decreased efficiency.

Wooden propellers are probably best if you don't break them often or can afford to break them. They deform very little, give excellent performance, and do less damage than other props (but still more than you'd volunteer for) if they hit your hand.

The third and most popular props at our field are made of black, glass-filled nylon. These give excellent perform-ance and usually survive rough landings, although they do have a few disadvantages. For example, the edges on a new prop are sharp. Sand these edges smooth before use but be aware that even after sanding a glass-filled nylon prop will do more damage if it strikes your hand than a wooden prop.

Also, because it is black, a glass-filled prop becomes invisible at high rpm. For this reason, paint the tips yellow, orange, or white so you don't forget where they are and put your hand into the meat grinder. Don't laugh; many of us have scars to show for that mental slip.

Finally, because they are so durable, glass-filled props are often used long

(Above) Before using a glass-filled nylon prop, sand the sharp edges. (Right) Then paint the tips a light color so you can see the prop when it's running.

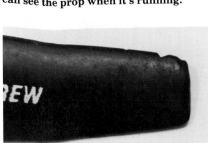

Eventually, the glass-filled prop gets nicked. When it does, use another.

after they should have been thrown away. If the blades are full of nicks or if you spot cracks, buy a new prop.

All in all, wooden props are probably best if you never land hard, ordinary nylon props are not recommended, and most people will settle for glass-filled nylon props such as those from Master Airscrew.

Choosing an RC system. The radio system consists of the transmitter, receiver, servos, batteries, and whatever switches, leads, and connectors are needed to tie the components together. Current systems are far more sophisticated than those of a few years ago, and because new features appear almost monthly, it is impossible to discuss all the choices you will have to make when you buy your radio equipment. The best I can do is to tell you to keep your first system reasonably simple, point out what you shouldn't buy, and mention special features you may find useful.

What not to buy; equipment you *don't* need:

1. Systems that use dry cells; some of this equipment is still on the market — don't buy it. If you inherit such equipment, convert to nicads before you use it. Dry cells are cheap but will soon run you into the poorhouse because you need new cells after each flying session. To convert to nicads, usually all you have to do is buy and plug in the appropriate nicad battery packs. Nicads are more expensive initially but far

cheaper in the long run because they can be recharged 500 to 1,000 times.

2. Equipment using 27 or 49 MHz frequencies, all 75 MHz (surface only) frequencies, and unless you have a ham license, all 50 and 53 MHz frequencies. The 27 MHz band is full of interference; the 49 MHz band is not only subject to interference, but because of legal limits on transmitter power it doesn't give adequate range to safely control an airplane; the 75 MHz frequencies are only for surface vehicles. They are illegal in planes, and if you use them, chances are some kid with a toy car will shoot you down, possibly hurting someone and definitely hurting your plane. The 50 and 53 MHz frequencies are legal only if you hold the appropriate amateur radio operator's license.

The FCC has assigned RC pilots the exclusive use of a large number of 72 MHz frequencies. It has also sandwiched pagers, crane operators, and other commercial users between RC frequencies. This means your receiver has to be very selective to reject signals from those sources. It also means your transmitter should produce a narrow band signal so you don't interfere with anyone else. Use only equipment on the 72 MHz band, but make sure it's designed to operate in this crowded radio spectrum. There is equipment on the market advertised as "1991 certified." Make sure that's the kind you get — and be sure it's on one of the 72 MHz "aircraft only" frequencies.

3. Two- or three-channel equipment. You will quickly progress to the point where you will want more channels. Even if your first plane uses only two or three, buy equipment that provides four or more channels.

4. Servo reversers. Let me hedge a bit here. Servo reversing switches make life much easier when you install controls. It's often easier to install a servo so that it moves the pushrod in the direction opposite the one you need than to install it so the control moves in the right direction. If you don't have servo reversers, you may have to fiddle for hours to get the servo installed properly. If you do have them, you just go ahead and install the servo any old way and flip a switch to change its direction of motion, if necessary. So far, so good.

The problem arises when you've been in the hobby a while and are flying two or more planes from the same transmitter. Chances are each plane requires different servo reverser switch positions, which means you'd best never slip up on a preflight when you change planes.

There is some danger involved. For example, if you get both throttle and rudder backwards, you could easily lose control while trying to taxi and perhaps hurt someone. A more likely prospect, though, is to take off with re-

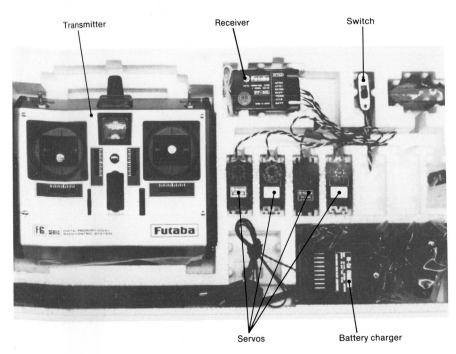

Transmitter   Receiver   Switch

Servos   Battery charger

I recommend that you begin with at least a four-channel RC system; a six-channel system such as this Futaba 6FGK is even better because you'll be able to use the extra channels on the more complex planes you'll build and fly later.

Here I'm charging the battery in a Futaba T6FN transmitter, a six-channel model that's a good choice for either beginner or expert.

versed ailerons. I've seen this happen several times, always with the same result. The plane takes off normally and the pilot makes the usual corrections with his ailerons. The plane rolls the wrong way. The pilot reflexively increases aileron control in the wrong direction. The plane rolls over and plows into the ground. If you must use servo reversers, never skip a preflight.

Equipment worth considering. The basic radio system will have a transmitter with at least four channels, will be powered by nicad batteries, and will have two joysticks. Ideally, it will also have a place to plug in a buddy cord and will be compatible with your instructor's system. Now for the bells and whistles:

1. An extra couple of channels can be nice, although most sport fliers use only four. You may want to add flaps, bomb-dropping capability, or retractable landing gear after you've become a proficient pilot.

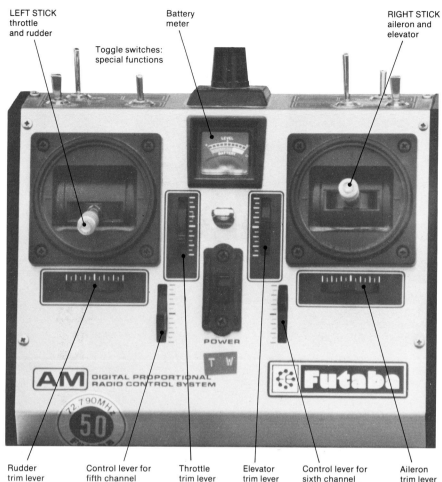

LEFT STICK throttle and rudder

Toggle switches: special functions

Battery meter

RIGHT STICK aileron and elevator

Rudder trim lever

Control lever for fifth channel

Throttle trim lever

Elevator trim lever

Control lever for sixth channel

Aileron trim lever

This is a fine transmitter, but you don't really need all the extra features controlled by the toggle switches on top, especially because all bets are off if you accidentally bump one while flying. Go with a simpler system for the time being.

2. Systems using pulse-code modulation (PCM): These code the radio signal so that the receiver preferentially recognizes your transmitter's signal over other signals on the same frequency. If you can get one at a reasonable price, it's probably worth having.

3. A neck strap: Most RC pilots in our area don't use them but should because the strap guarantees that if your hand slips the transmitter will still be there for you to grab — not down on the ground sending suicidal signals to your airplane.

Single-stick transmitters such as this seven-channel Airtronics CS7PS are excellent if you can find an instructor who's accustomed to such rigs, but you'll probably end up with two sticks.

If you have a bent for electronics, you may eventually want to customize a radio control system, perhaps by adding a keyboard to control an almost unlimited number of functions.

The transmitter can't fall to the ground if you wear a neck strap.

The S16 servo on the left cost more than the S23 on the right, but was well worth it.

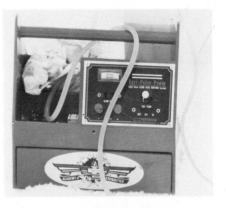

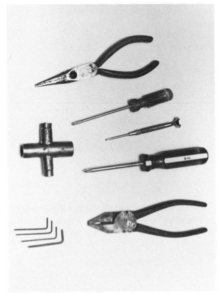

These simple hand tools are all you need at the field. The cross-shaped object is a four-way socket wrench for tightening and loosening such items as glow plugs and prop nuts.

(Top and above) Buy or make a field box just large enough to hold a lead-acid battery (often a 12-volt motorcycle battery), a fuel container and pump, a few tools and spare parts, a power panel, and possibly an electric starter. Large field boxes are impressive but heavy.

Servos. Finally, a few words about buying servos. You need four, but some four-channel radio systems are sold with three servos to keep the apparent price down. If you buy one of those sets, you're going to have to buy another servo, so add that to the price as you do your comparison shopping.

Often, radio manufacturers offer a choice of servos, and my experience is that it's best to get the more expensive ones. For instance, when I began flying RC, Futaba offered radio systems that were virtually identical except that the less expensive one came with S-26 servos and the more expensive one came with S-16s. I bought both systems. The S-16 servos, as I recall, cost about ten dollars more each, and were easily worth twice that difference. They performed yeoman service and responded quickly and accurately to the slightest stick pressure. The S-26s worked the controls, but not quite as cleanly. Moreover, their potentiometers required frequent cleaning and they wore out faster than the S-16s. If you have a choice, buy the system with the better (and usually more expensive) servos.

One last note on servos: Not all are compatible with your radio system. In fact, some of the servos from a particular manufacturer may not even be compatible with all of that manufacturer's radio systems. The servos that come with your system will be okay, but make absolutely sure that any you buy separately will, in fact, work with your equipment.

I've listed the most important information you need to buy a good radio system, but there is no substitute for experience. Before you buy, go to the field and see what seems to work for others.

Field equipment. After you've taken care of the radio gear, you'll need field equipment, beginning with a field box. Many modelers design and build their own, with elaborate piping and electrical systems. You'll find such things at the flying field, and there's no reason you can't design one for yourself. There is, however, one reason not to: If you build a 70-pound service station, you're going to have to carry it.

I suggest you keep it small. I even suggest you buy a commercial field box from a hobby shop or mail-order house to save time. The box need only be big enough to carry the small amount of equipment necessary to fly and service your plane at the field. The heavy items will be a gallon container of fuel, an electric starter, and the battery to power the plug-in accessories. All told, the box plus equipment should weigh about 25 pounds. Here's what you need:

1. A large 12-volt battery: A motorcycle battery will do fine. In conjunction with the power panel it will be used to run the starter and fuel pump, to heat the glow plug, and if you have a field charger, to recharge the radio batteries. You will also need a small charger for the 12-volt battery.

2. A power panel: The power panel is the heart of your field box. It connects to the 12-volt battery and distributes power to the electrical accessories — the starter, the glow plug, and the fuel pump. You can easily get by with the cheapest available, but if you want a fancy panel, talk with a flier who already owns one to see if it's worth the extra cost.

3. Field tools: You'll need standard and needle-nose pliers; a set of small allen wrenches to tighten wheel collars, engine mounts, and so forth; a va-

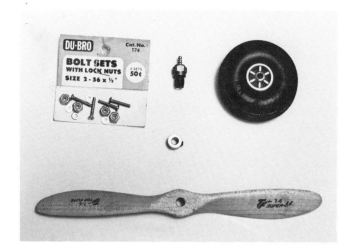

You don't need many spare parts in your field box, either. In fact, you can usually get by with just a couple of extra props and a glow plug. The other items are handy, but optional.

An electric starter is a good investment. The Ni-Starter (lower right) is a rechargeable nickel-cadmium cell that can be used to start the engine away from the field box.

Take along glass cleaner and paper towels to remove grease and dirt from the plane after a flying session.

The fuel pump, usually attached to the fuel can, doesn't look like much, but you need it. This one is electric; manual pumps are also available.

The power panel, the heart of the field box, delivers electricity from the battery to the starter, glow plug, and fuel pump.

riety of screwdrivers, mostly small, several with Phillips heads; and a prop wrench.

4. Spare parts: Take along nuts, bolts, and screws to replace any that might come loose, and a spare wheel and wheel collar. You should also carry an extra glow plug and enough propellers so you don't have to cease flying for lack of a prop. If you use glass-filled props, one spare should do. If you use wood, carry half a dozen, at least during your novice days.

5. A two-ounce plastic syringe: This is handy for priming engines and clearing plugged fuel systems. In a pinch, it will also do as a fuel pump.

6. An electric starter: It's possible to fly without one, but especially in cold weather, or if you use a four-cycle engine, you'll want one. It will make starting easier and keep your hand

clear of the prop, out of harm's way.

7. A glow plug clip and leads: There are a variety of glow plug clips on the market. Pick one that locks onto the plug. Otherwise the prop may snap off a loose clip and throw it into your face.

You may want to try a McDaniel R/C Ni-Starter or Ace R/C Nilite II: Each is a small nicad that locks onto the glow plug, allowing you to start the engine even if you're away from the field box.

8. A fuel pump: You'll need some kind of pump to get fuel from the can or plastic bottle into the airplane's tank. Some people prefer manual pumps, some like electrics. Both do the job and neither is expensive.

9. Rubber bands: A box of rubber bands of whatever size (usually No. 64) is required to keep the wings on your plane. Don't use rubber bands for more than a week or two. If they show signs of fatigue before that, replace them.

10. Cleaning materials: Model airplane engines spit oil all over the plane. You have to clean the model before you can put it back into the car, so be sure when you leave for the field that you're toting a roll of paper towels and a bottle of window cleaner.

You may have noticed that I didn't mention fast-curing epoxies or cyanoacrylate instant glues. By and large, I think it's a mistake to fix even minor crash damage at the field. The urge to fly is too great and the damage is often more extensive than it first appears. Take the plane home, inspect it at leisure, and do the job right.

If you've assembled all the tools and equipment I've mentioned, you won't be the best-equipped guy in the club, but you'll have enough to fly consistently. You can add to the collection as inclination and finances dictate.

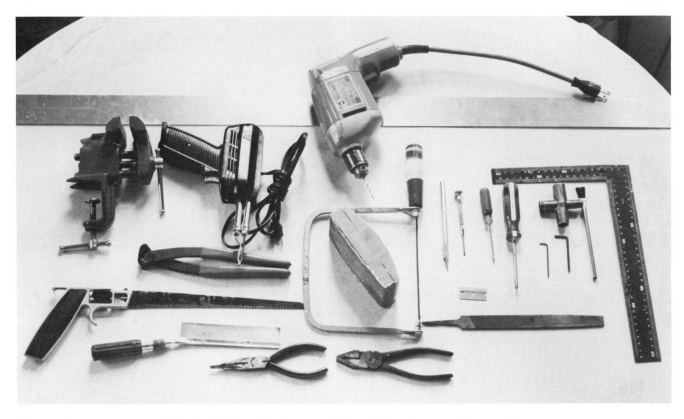

These tools were enough to build the Goldberg Eaglet and will be sufficient for most other models.

3. Building the airplane

This chapter is not a substitute for your kit's instruction booklet; it is intended only to list the items you'll need to build your model and to help you avoid the most common beginner's mistakes. First of all, you'll be happy to learn that you don't need an elaborate workshop or fancy tools to build a model plane. A well-equipped workshop does make the job easier, but you can do without it. The Eaglet, Box Fly, and Ranger shown in this chapter were all built on a kitchen table, and I once built a seven-foot wing on a credenza.

All you really need is a flat working surface.

Tools and materials. The requirements for tools are nearly as simple. In building the Eaglet I used a 48″ metal straightedge, soldering gun, power drill, vise, hacksaw, coping saw, razor saw, modeling knife, single-edge razor blade, sanding block and sandpaper, carpenter's square, rattail file, small and medium Phillips screwdrivers, small conventional screwdriver, standard and needle-nose pliers, .050″ and ³⁄₃₂″ allen wrenches, Z-bender pliers, four-way

prop wrench, epoxy brush, and flatiron.

To complete the Eaglet, I bought a variety of accessories which together cost slightly more than the kit itself. As a result, the Eaglet cost only a few dollars less to put into the air than the Box Fly, a more complete kit. The additional items were wheels and wheel collars, fuel tank and line, 4-40 bolts and locknuts, prop spinner, pushrod connectors, flexible pushrod cable, foam rubber, thread, No. 64 rubber bands, straight pins, 5-minute epoxy glue, Hobbypoxy 2 epoxy, Titebond aliphatic resin glue, Zap-a-gap cyanoacrylate instant glue, silicone rubber, and Pactra Solarfilm iron-on, heat-shrink plastic covering material.

Having assembled the materials, you will want to build your plane strong enough to hold together in the air and stand up to hard landings, but you can't make it crashproof, and if you try, you'll only add extra weight that will make a crash more likely. Don't spare the glue on joints, but wipe off the excess before it dries because it adds weight.

Silk and dope covering is strong and pretty, but takes forever to apply and, unless you're careful, adds weight. For that first trainer, you'll be better off with a strong, lightweight plastic covering material such as Solarfilm.

Preventing structural failure. Assuming you don't add gobs of epoxy or paint or extra bracing, your plane should turn out light enough, but there are a variety of errors that can make entry into the hobby a trial. Some mis-

Use lots of rubber bands (16 is not too many) to hold the wing onto the fuselage. Cross the last two to prevent the others from slipping off.

takes will detract from the plane's performance, others can cause structural failure in flight.

One of the most spectacular crashes happens when the wing comes off in flight. The fuselage, usually with the engine wide open, follows an ever steeper trajectory toward the ground, moving much faster than it would in an ordinary power dive because there is no drag from the wing to slow it down. Inevitably, it goes straight in, digs a deep hole in the ground, and demolishes itself. The time from wing separation to crash is no more than three seconds. For those seconds, there is the screaming engine and the awful knowledge of doom. Then there is near silence, often heightened by the waspish sound of another plane still in the air. Everyone instinctively looks back to the sky, where the wing tumbles gently toward earth. It takes the wing a long time to land.

Almost always the reason for the crash is too few rubber bands or rubber bands that slipped off the dowels that were supposed to hold them in place. To prevent this catastrophe, use lots of rubber bands, cross the last two as shown in the photo, and make the dowels long enough that no matter how greasy the rubber bands become (and they get very greasy) they can't slip off. I use 16 No. 64 rubber bands on a four- or five-pound airplane — seven on each side and two crossed over. This may be excessive, but it's safe.

Unfortunately, some models come with dowels that are too short to hold that many rubber bands. If yours is one of those, discard the original dowels and install your own. The dowels should project about ¾" from the fuselage side. The Box Fly comes with bolt-on "dowels" that won't hold enough rubber bands to make me happy, so one of the first things I did was replace them with wooden dowels. The fact that the Box Fly was not designed for dowels that go completely through the fuselage complicated this change by forcing me to use four short dowels instead of two long ones. I installed the new dowels

and braced them with ¼" plywood triangles epoxied to the inside of the fuselage.

Another spectacular crash happens when the wing folds up in flight. The break usually occurs in the center section, so build that part as strong as you reasonably can. On many models there is no spar joining the wing halves; instead, tremendous strength is built in by reinforcing the center section with epoxy and fiberglass cloth. A few kits

Wing hold-down dowels should protrude about ¾".

The original "dowels" on the Box Fly were too short for my taste, so I replaced them with sturdy wooden dowels reinforced inside the fuselage with triangles of ¼" plywood.

rely solely on spars to hold the wing halves together. Spars are fine, but sometimes snap, so fiberglass the center section even if the kit instructions don't call for it. Brush a thick coat of epoxy over the wood, then lay the fiberglass cloth in place over it and smooth out all wrinkles and bubbles. Then put a thin coat of epoxy over the top of the glass cloth and squeegee off the excess with a piece of cardboard like that used for tablet backs.

Hinge failure is another major cause of crashes. If an aileron comes loose in flight, you stand a good chance of crashing; if an elevator comes loose, it will take magic to land safely. The recommended way to secure a hinge is to pin it with a round wooden toothpick. First install the hinge in the prescribed way, then drill a hole through the control surface so that it passes through the hinge. Epoxy a toothpick into the hole, cut it off even with the surface, and sand it smooth.

Preventing control surface flutter. Failed hinges have caused many a crash, but even if the hinges hold, there's a related problem to worry about — flutter. Some time ago, I was instructing a student who had an RCM 60 with a high-powered Webra engine and a tuned pipe. The plane was so overpowered that after a ten-foot take-off run it could point its nose straight up and climb out of sight in seconds. Once he got the hang of the thing, my student loved to fly it full bore. He was

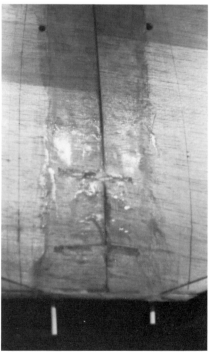

Strengthen the wing center section with fiberglass cloth and epoxy. I got away with a sloppy (but strong) job on this Bonanza wing center section, which will be hidden. This area will be exposed on your trainer, so apply the cloth more smoothly for better appearance.

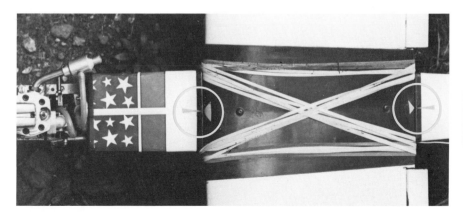

Mark the wing and fuselage centers (circled here) so you can align the wing easily. These rubber bands are old and frayed — use new ones for actual flying.

Neither tail surface boasts a great finish, but the one on the left has an enormous hinge gap that could lead to flutter. The one on the right has almost no gap and is less likely to cause trouble. All control surfaces must move freely, but there must be no unwanted play in the pushrods or cables linking each surface and its servo.

doing fine until the plane began to wallow.

At that point he handed me the transmitter, and with some difficulty, I managed to land the plane. On the ground, the problem was obvious. The right aileron had snapped about three or four inches from the fuselage. We had heard flutter (which sounds like a bull-roarer) just before the aileron gave way. If you ever hear flutter on your plane, chop the throttle and land im-

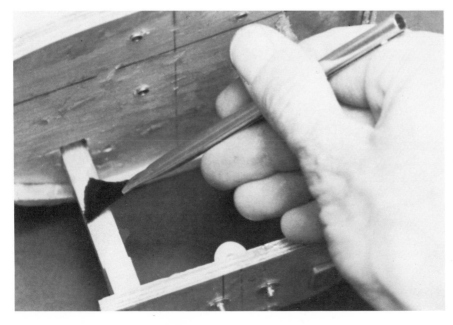

Use at least the number of hinges specified; pin each with a toothpick.

Brush on epoxy to seal all wood surfaces that will be exposed to fuel.

mediately. A second's delay may be too much.

There are several ways to prevent flutter — use a smaller engine, decrease the gap between wing and aileron or stab and elevator, install counterweights, install extra hinges, decrease the size of the flutter-prone control surface, or stiffen it with braces — and that just begins the list. Usually on trainers, though, the problem is either poor hinging or a loose aileron torque rod, and the solution is simple.

If you hear flutter and manage to land safely, check the plane carefully. If any hinge line (the gap between control surface and the surface it's hinged to) is more than $\frac{1}{16}''$, remove the hinges, and after making sure that the two surfaces are properly mated, install new hinges, leaving as small a gap as possible. This is a miserable, tedious job, but the alternative is an almost certain crash.

If the problem is with an aileron, check it for excessive play. If you can move it up or down appreciably without also moving the servo, the torque rod has probably worked loose inside the aileron. Cut out a section from the underside of the aileron, exposing the torque rod. Fill any cavity with epoxy, then replace the piece of aileron you originally removed and wait for the epoxy to cure.

Both of these sources of flutter can be avoided as you build. First, before hinging the control surfaces, sand them until they exactly match the surfaces to which they will be hinged. Then install the hinges so that the gap is no more than $\frac{1}{16}''$ (preferably less). Second, when installing the aileron torque rods, drill oversize holes for them and fill those holes with epoxy before pressing the rods into place. This will prevent play from developing.

Engine installation tips. The front of the fuselage is under unremitting attack from vibration and hot fuel, a combination that can weaken wood and glue joints. The best way to thwart this attack is to epoxy any area that will be

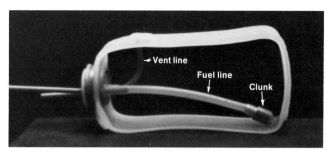

I cut this fuel tank apart to demonstrate properly arranged fuel and vent lines. The weighted end (the clunk) of the fuel line is free to move and the vent line extends into the molded bubble at the top of the tank.

I prefer glass-filled nylon engine mounts because they are strong and easy to use. Many sizes are available.

exposed to fuel with a slow-curing formulation such as Hobbypoxy 2. Brush a thin coat of the epoxy over every nook and cranny that could conceivably be exposed to fuel. This includes the engine and fuel tank compartments, as well as any other place that might otherwise become fuel-soaked.

Before installing the engine, make sure every nut and bolt and screw on it is tight. Use discretion, though, because you don't want to strip any threads. Be especially careful with the screws or bolts that hold the carburetor in place.

There are three common kinds of engine mounts. Those on the Eaglet are wooden and I don't like them because they are subject to wear from engine vibration, become fuel-soaked too easily, and are difficult to repair. However, rather then redesign the front end of the fuselage, I used them, and you probably will, too, if you build an Eaglet.

The Box Fly came with an aluminum engine mount already installed. I don't like these, either, partly because they can be difficult to drill and partly because in a crash they sometimes prove stronger than the engine.

Along with many other modelers, I prefer a glass-filled nylon mount. It stands up to vibration and fuel, is easy to drill, and breaks in a crash, usually leaving the engine undamaged.

You will have to attach an aluminum or glass-filled mount to the fire wall. Many mounts come with wood screws for that purpose, but don't use them because sooner or later they would vibrate loose. Hold the mount to the fire wall with bolts and blind nuts. As an added precaution, I usually coat the bolts with epoxy before installation. You can still remove the bolts later if need be but the epoxy prevents the bolts from removing themselves.

Once the mount is drilled and bolted on the fire wall, mounting the engine is straightforward. Just be sure to use the proper bolt size and tighten the bolts in place with locknuts. Forget about ordinary nuts with lock washers; they come loose too easily.

Installing the fuel system. There is nothing challenging about installing the fuel system, but if you do it wrong, you will have all sorts of headaches.

The standard fuel tank is essentially a plastic bottle. Fuel is drawn out through a flexible line which is kept at the bottom of the tank by a weight called a clunk. The manufacturer's instructions will tell you how to assemble the tank, but here are a few extra pointers. First, before you install the tank in your plane, be sure the clunk works. If it's too far back in the tank or if the fuel line to which the clunk is attached is too stiff, it will not move freely. The clunk should immediately sink to the lowest point as you rotate the tank around its horizontal axis in any direction. If it hangs up because it's touching the back of the tank, shorten the flexible line. If it has clearance and still won't drop, the line is too stiff. Get a more flexible line from the hobby store.

When installing the tank, place it so that the center of the tank is ½″ or so below the needle valve. If it is much

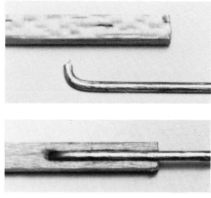

If you decide to use wooden pushrods, here's how to secure the rod to its wire. First bend the wire 90 degrees as shown at top. Next cut a hole and groove in the wood to accept the wire. Then remove the wire, fill the hole and groove with epoxy, replace the wire, and wrap the assembly with carpet thread.

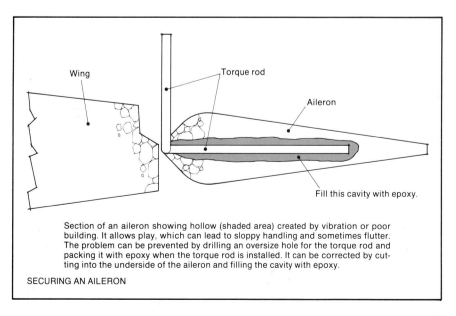

Section of an aileron showing hollow (shaded area) created by vibration or poor building. It allows play, which can lead to sloppy handling and sometimes flutter. The problem can be prevented by drilling an oversize hole for the torque rod and packing it with epoxy when the torque rod is installed. It can be corrected by cutting into the underside of the aileron and filling the cavity with epoxy.

SECURING AN AILERON

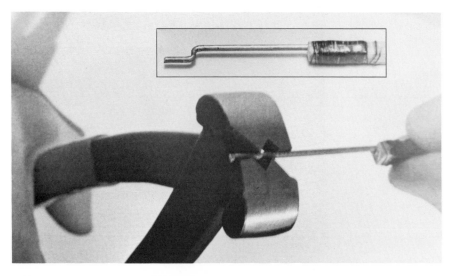

I like to use a Z-bender pliers such as this one from Hobby Shack to bend wire pushrods. The technique is simple and inexpensive. Install a Goldberg, Du-Bro, or some other brand of threaded clevis (called a quick link), pushrod keeper, or a similar device at the control horn end of the pushrod to permit trim adjustments.

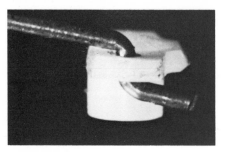

Observe how the Z-bend slips into place so that it can't work itself loose.

Pushrod connectors and flexible cable inside a plastic sleeve are handy for hooking up the throttle and nosewheel.

higher than this, fuel will tend to siphon into the carburetor when the engine is stopped, resulting in a flooded engine that will not start easily. When you go to a hotter plane and spend considerable time flying inverted, you will want the tank even with the needle

valve and you'll just have to live with the flooding. It will be a while before you intentionally fly inverted, so locate the tank a little below the needle valve.

When installing the tank, make sure that it does not contact anything hard, especially anything that is also sharp.

Sharp objects will eventually punch holes in your tank; contact between the tank and any rigid structure will transmit engine vibration and cause foaming, which will give you fits when tuning the engine. Cut off any protruding bolts that might touch the tank and surround the tank with foam rubber to isolate it from vibration.

When you install the fuel tank and muffler, ensure an airtight seal by using the smallest diameter tubing that will fit. Loose lines allow air to seep in and cause erratic engine performance. Also, make the lines as short and straight as possible and don't let them touch the engine except at the fittings. If you're not certain that the lines are tight enough, replace them with the next smaller diameter.

On most models there will be two holes in the fire wall for lines from the tank. When installing the tank, drill both of these ¼″ or so oversize. After the tank is installed, but before you attach the flexible fuel lines to the metal tubes protruding from the tank, seal the metal lines in place by surrounding them with silicone rubber (don't use epoxy; it's too rigid). The silicone will keep fuel out of the tank compartment and help isolate the tank from vibration.

Pushrods. Making pushrods is easy enough, but can cost you a plane if you do it wrong. The photos show the right way. Keep the metal parts of the pushrods as short and straight as possible. Otherwise the rods will flex excessively under pressure — as when trying to pull out of a dive! Also, use Z-bends to link the aileron, rudder, and elevator pushrods to their servos. Most people use pushrod connectors, but Z-bends are safer. However, for connecting throttle and nosewheel pushrods, you can use pushrod connectors because failure of these controls will not automatically cause a crash.

Throttle and nose gear pushrods are usually just steel cables sliding through plastic sheaths; this allows you to snake your pushrods through tight places in the radio and fuel tank compartments. It also allows some play so that when the nosewheel takes a hard bump, as it will, the servo is not likely to be damaged.

Some modelers use flexible pushrod systems in which a plastic (usually nylon) rod runs inside a plastic sleeve, but I don't recommend these if there is any alternative because the plastic expands and contracts appreciably with temperature changes, necessitating frequent retrimming.

Once your pushrods are installed, check to make sure all control surfaces move freely. If you hear a scraping or clicking when you move the control surface, or if the response is slow, correct the problem before flying. I once had a model that clicked faintly when I moved the aileron control. It flew beau-

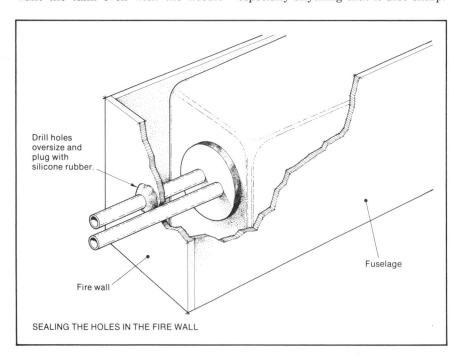

Drill holes oversize and plug with silicone rubber.

Fuselage

Fire wall

SEALING THE HOLES IN THE FIRE WALL

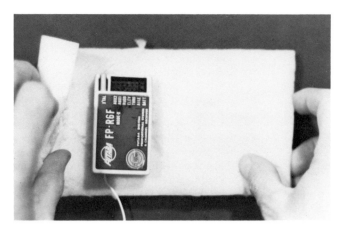

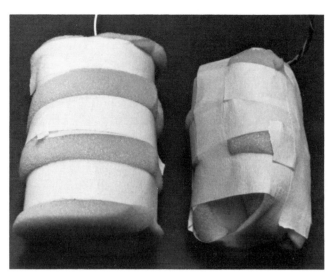

Wrap the receiver and battery pack in plenty of foam rubber and secure both inside the fuselage where they can't shift about regardless of the plane's position.

tifully for more than 100 flights, but one day the ailerons hung up and the plane began rolling. All I could do was alternately push up and down elevator to maintain altitude. Fortunately, the aileron managed to free itself before the plane was out of sight and I landed safely. I repaired the model that evening, but failure to do so earlier nearly cost me a plane.

Ailerons have no monopoly on hanging up. Rudders and elevators can also freeze and wreck your plane. Even if a surface doesn't hang up, it will increase the load on the battery if it doesn't move freely; this could leave you 200 feet up with no radio. Fix it before you take off.

Model engines cause lots of vibration, which has a way of destroying electrical connections. If you've been around the flying field a while, you know that receivers fail occasionally, but transmitters almost never do. The difference is vibration and the way to protect your receiver and battery is to wrap them in plenty of foam rubber, secured with tape. If the tape is too tight, it will compress the foam and defeat the purpose of the padding, so wrap the tape just tightly enough to keep the foam in place. Use as much foam rubber as you can fit into the plane.

Securing the receiver and battery. The demise of the Stinson SR-9 shown here reminds me to mention that the receiver and battery must be fastened inside the plane so they cannot move regardless of the plane's attitude. The Stinson was a beautifully designed and constructed model and it flew like the real thing.

Unfortunately, the pilot (who was not the owner) decided to roll it, unaware that the receiver was simply lying inside the fuselage with only gravity to hold it in place. All went well until the plane got to the upside-down part of the roll. Then the receiver fell, pulling out the lead that connected it to the elevator servo. The big Stinson was reduced to rubble about three seconds

later. Moral of the story: Dab a little silicone rubber on the tape that holds the foam around the receiver and battery and stick your electronic components to a piece of wood inside the airplane so they can't fall and cause a crash.

When installing servos, make sure they are protected from vibration. Use the rubber grommets that came with the radio system and be sure not to tighten them so much that they are totally compressed — just enough to hold a little tension on the bolts (or screws, if you must use screws). If you squash the grommets down tightly, they will transmit the vibration they were intended to absorb.

The importance of correct alignment and balance. One of the first planes I built was a hot .049 ½A. Fortunately, since I was a novice, I asked an expert to fly it for me. Like most ½As this one had no throttle; the engine was wide open for the entire eight-minute flight — eight minutes of terror, it turned out. My expert was perspiring heavily when he finally got the plane down in one piece. The prob-

lem was that just to fly level, he had to hold almost full down elevator and full right aileron.

Back on the ground, we soon found the source of the plane's bizarre flight characteristics — I had misaligned both the horizontal and vertical stabilizers, which is not easy to do. Misalignment of the horizontal stab takes a special talent because the die-cut fuselage parts on many kits force it into correct alignment. I had somehow managed to defeat this safeguard.

Some kits (the Eaglet and the Box Fly among them) are constructed to force the vertical stabilizer into proper alignment also, but this is not foolproof. To avoid misalignment, draw a center line on your fuselage early in its construction. Just mark the center of the fuselage top somewhere near the tail and somewhere near the rear of the wing saddle and use a straightedge to draw a line through those two points.

When you're ready to install the fin, first apply slow-curing epoxy — not the 5-minute kind — to both surfaces to be joined. Then pin them together so that the fin is exactly lined up with the cen-

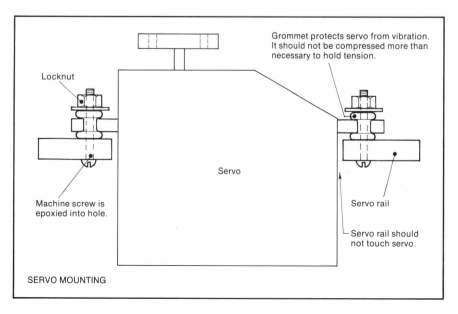

Grommet protects servo from vibration. It should not be compressed more than necessary to hold tension.

Locknut

Machine screw is epoxied into hole.

Servo

Servo rail

Servo rail should not touch servo.

SERVO MOUNTING

ter line. To be absolutely sure you've got it straight, place your straightedge flush with one side of the fin and see whether it runs parallel to the center line. If it doesn't, move the fin around till it does. When you're satisfied, pin it securely, making sure it is exactly square with the horizontal stabilizer. Check one more time, and if all is well, leave it alone until the epoxy cures.

Another source of poor flying characteristics is wing warp. Even if you build carefully on a flat surface the wing can twist when you iron on the covering. If the total warp is more than ⅛", correct it before flying. To correct this kind of warp, twist the wing against the direction of warp, heat the covering with a flatiron or heat gun, and hold it in place until the covering cools. Check again for warps, and if necessary, repeat the operation until the wing is straight.

A special kind of warp occurs when two perfectly straight wing halves are joined a little out of alignment. This is easily preventable and should never happen to you. If it does, you will have to cut the wing in half at the center joint and reconnect it properly. Don't forget to cover the repaired center section with a new sheath of fiberglass and epoxy.

Now for the question of how to detect the warp in the first place. Most instructions on the subject tell you to eyeball it. The human eye has its merits, but since it can detect only gross warps, the safest procedure is to measure. I do this on every new plane and rarely have to move the aileron trim lever more than a click or two to achieve hands-off level flight.

Here's how to measure. Install the wing with a few rubber bands, set the plane on a level surface, and block the wheels with books so the plane can't move if you bump it. Then, using a carpenter's square, measure from points A

This beautiful Stinson Reliant, taking off on one of its last flights, was lost because the leads connecting the receiver and servos became disconnected while the plane was performing aerobatic maneuvers.

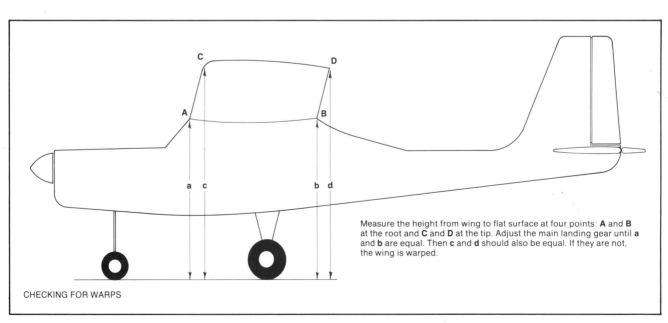

Measure the height from wing to flat surface at four points: **A** and **B** at the root and **C** and **D** at the tip. Adjust the main landing gear until **a** and **b** are equal. Then **c** and **d** should also be equal. If they are not, the wing is warped.

CHECKING FOR WARPS

Draw a center line on the fuselage and line up everything with it. If you build straight, your plane will fly straight. If you don't, it may not fly at all.

Balance the plane before taking it to the field. A tail-heavy plane is unflyable.

and B to the surface the plane rests on. Adjust the main gear until A and B are equal. Next, measure C and D. If they are not also equal, the wing is warped. If the difference is more than ⅛", straighten out the warp before flying.

There is an exception to this rule. If your wing is designed with washout, both panels will be intentionally warped by the same amount. That is, D will be longer than C by the same amount on both wing panels. However, if C is longer than D, you do not have washout, but a particularly treacherous kind of warp that should be corrected before you attempt to fly the plane.

If the first wing panel is straight, measure the second before you move the plane. It should also be straight. If A and B are equal on the second panel, but C and D are not, you have an ordinary warp. If A and B differ by ⅛" or more, the panels are seriously misaligned and you will have to cut the wing in half, as described earlier, to correct the problem. Check your measurements several times before doing this. It is not fun.

While not as critical as wing alignment, it is important to build the fuselage straight. That's easy enough to do, but there are a few places where extra care will pay off. For one thing, build over the plans, making sure the whole fuselage fits exactly over the drawing. If you get it crooked, it's going to fly crooked. The plane may fly well enough once you get it trimmed out, but if nothing else, it will look funny because even in a dead calm, it won't quite fly in the direction the nose points.

Installing the fire wall requires special care, not only because it takes a beating from vibration, but because on most models, the engine mount bolts directly to it. The angle at which the fire wall and fuselage meet determines the thrust line of the engine, which can make the difference between a great-flying airplane and a dog. Most trainers require right thrust and down thrust. The right thrust is to counter the engine's torque, the down thrust to minimize the tendency of high-wing airplanes to climb when power is applied. Follow the kit instructions meticulously, and if you get the thrust line wrong, correct the error before flying.

When your plane is finished, with the spinner and prop and everything else but the fuel installed, check the balance point. It should be right where the instructions say it should be. If the plane is ¼" or less nose-heavy, don't worry about it, but if it's more nose-heavy than that, fix it. Otherwise you may end up with a sluggish plane that is hard to flare on landing.

If the plane is even slightly tail-heavy, fix it. Tail-heavy airplanes are sensitive, which is not what you need right now, and if the plane is very tail-heavy, not even the best pilot can fly it. When in doubt, remember that nose-heavy beats tail-heavy every time.

The preferred way to shift the balance point is to rearrange radio equipment inside the fuselage. Try that first, but if it's not enough, add tail or nose weights as needed — and make sure the weights can't come off in flight, leaving you with an unflyable plane. You can buy lead weights from the local hobby shop, or can use washers,

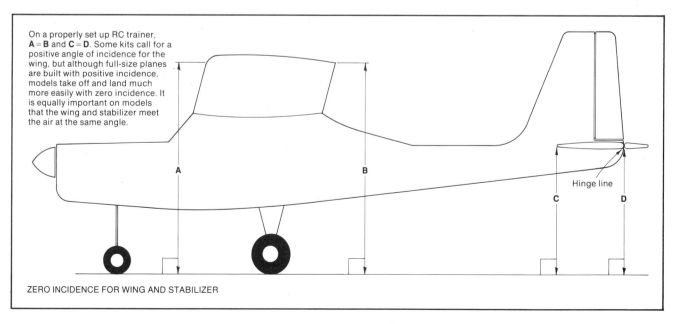

On a properly set up RC trainer, **A** = **B** and **C** = **D**. Some kits call for a positive angle of incidence for the wing, but although full-size planes are built with positive incidence, models take off and land much more easily with zero incidence. It is equally important on models that the wing and stabilizer meet the air at the same angle.

A   B

Hinge line

C   D

ZERO INCIDENCE FOR WING AND STABILIZER

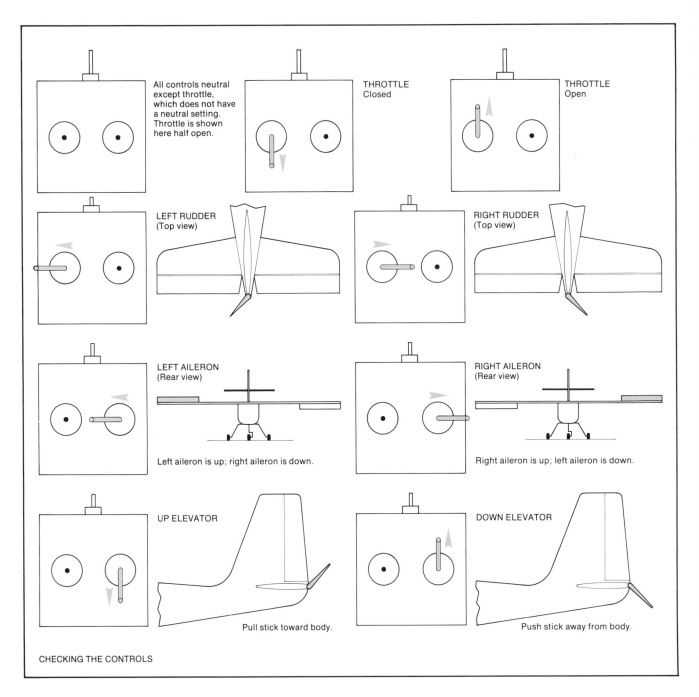

All controls neutral except throttle, which does not have a neutral setting. Throttle is shown here half open.

THROTTLE Closed

THROTTLE Open

LEFT RUDDER (Top view)

RIGHT RUDDER (Top view)

LEFT AILERON (Rear view)

Left aileron is up; right aileron is down.

RIGHT AILERON (Rear view)

Right aileron is up; left aileron is down.

UP ELEVATOR

Pull stick toward body.

DOWN ELEVATOR

Push stick away from body.

CHECKING THE CONTROLS

sinkers, tire weights, or other pieces of metal. I've even balanced planes by epoxying quarters to the fuselage.

Now make sure the landing gear is properly set up. If you haven't already done so, limit nosewheel response by connecting the steering cable to the outermost hole on the steering arm. There's no need for quick turns on the ground and an inadvertent one can re-kit your plane.

Next, check again that the wings are at zero incidence when the plane sits on a flat surface. If the wings sit at a positive angle when the plane rolls along the ground, they will decrease the weight on the wheels during the take-off run, reducing nosewheel effectiveness before airspeed is high enough for good rudder control. Worse, the plane may pop into the air before it's ready to fly, an event often followed by a cart-

wheel and hours of repair work. You can adjust the angle of incidence of the wing by bending the main landing gear to raise or lower the center of the fuselage.

While you're at it, check the incidence of the horizontal stabilizer. It should also be zero. If it is not, correct it to prevent trim problems in the air.

If you have an incidence meter, an angle finder adapted for use with model planes, by all means use it. If not, just measure. Measuring takes longer, but works just as well.

Now make sure the rudder and nosewheel track together. Set the rudder trim tab to the neutral position, give the plane a shove, and see if it follows a straight track. If it doesn't, adjust the nosewheel mechanically (not with the trim tab) until it does. Do this before you leave the house because it's impos-

sible to set the nosewheel accurately on a bumpy outdoor surface.

Check the controls one more time. The rudder should move to the left side of the plane when you push the rudder stick to the left, and the nose gear should rotate counterclockwise as seen from above. The opposite, of course, is true for right rudder. The throttle control should open the engine's venturi when pushed away and close it when pulled toward the body (or down). The elevator should rise when the stick is pulled toward you and go down when the stick is pushed away. When you give left aileron, the left aileron should come up and the right aileron should go down.

Finally, center the trim tabs and make sure that all control surfaces return to neutral when you let go of the transmitter sticks.

As on this Box Fly, you can sometimes convert a sport plane to a trainer by increasing the area of the wing and stab.

4. Taming a hot airplane

Some of you will have had the bad luck to come into possession of an airplane that is too hot for a beginner to handle. If it's a scale P-51 or almost anything except a high-wing plane that weighs too much for the wing, this chapter won't help you, but if your plane would be a good trainer except that it flies too fast for a beginner, you can probably put training wheels on it by extending the wing and horizontal tail. This will make the plane look a little odd, but if it's still around after you've become an accomplished RC pilot you can remove the training wheels and restore its good looks.

Two cautions before you get started. First, if your wing has washout, don't do it. Second, if the wing is tapered or swept-back, don't modify it unless you know exactly what you're doing. If you simply extend such a wing, you'll move the center of lift and possibly end up with an unflyable plane.

If your plane is suitable for modification, your first task is to perform some calculations so that the wing and tail

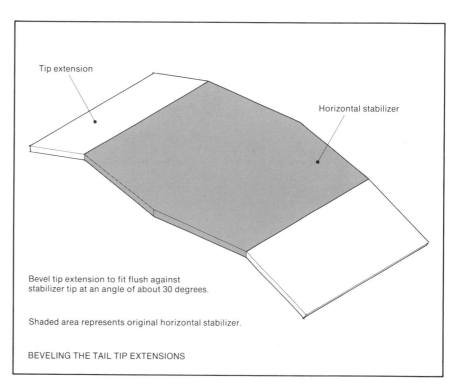

Tip extension

Horizontal stabilizer

Bevel tip extension to fit flush against
stabilizer tip at an angle of about 30 degrees.

Shaded area represents original horizontal stabilizer.

BEVELING THE TAIL TIP EXTENSIONS

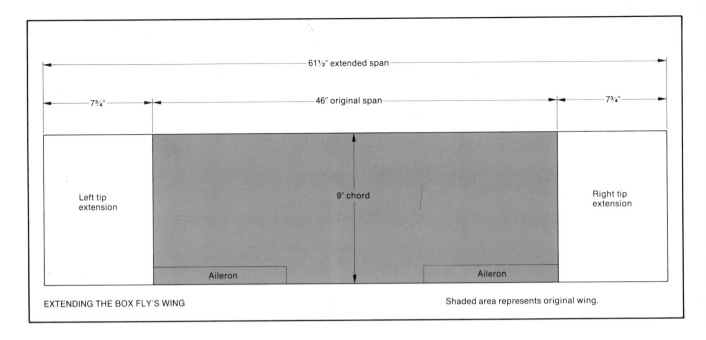

areas will come out right. To make these you'll first need to know the plane's weight in ounces, the original wingspan in inches, and the original wing area in square feet. If you have the wing area in square inches, divide by 144 to get square feet. For example, if the area is 414 square inches, divide 414 by 144 to get 2.875 square feet.

First calculate the length of the wing extension panels, represented by L in the formula below:

$$L = \frac{1}{2} \left(\frac{\text{Span} \times \text{Weight}}{17 \times \text{Area}} - \text{Span} \right)$$

Let's assume your plane's wingspan is 46 inches, the weight is 65 ounces, and the wing area is 414 square inches. First divide 414 by 144 to get the wing area in square feet, 2.875. Now plug into the formula:

$$L = \frac{1}{2} \left(\frac{46 \times 65}{17 \times 2.875} - 46 \right)$$

or L = ½ (61.176 − 46)
or L = ½ (15.176)
or L = 7.59 inches

Each wing extension, then, will add 7.59″ to the wingspan. For convenience, round up to 7¾″. Since the wing chord is 9″, each extension panel will be 9″ wide and 7¾″ long. When installed, these extensions will increase the wing area in this example by 34 percent to 3.44 square feet. This will give a wing loading of 16.9 ounces per square foot if we ignore the weight of the extensions themselves. Since your wing will have different dimensions, your wing extenders will not be identical to the ones calculated here, but they will drop the wing loading to about 17 ounces per square foot.

You will also have to calculate the length of the tail extensions, a slightly more involved process. Unlike trainer wings, which are usually rectangular, tails are typically trapezoidal. For those whose math is a little rusty, I've worked out a formula. To make your own calculations, just substitute your plane's measurements for the ones I've used and get out your pocket calculator. If you have doubts, don't guess. Get help from someone with a mathematical bent.

For the tail used in this example, the original dimensions are given in the sketch and the following calculations are based on those dimensions. Yours, of course, will be different.

To calculate the original tail area, first add the root chord (5 inches in this case) and the tip chord (4 inches) and divide the sum by 2. That is,

$$\frac{5 + 4}{2} = \frac{9}{2} = 4.5$$

Next, multiply that answer by the tailspan (18.5 inches) to get the area (4.5 x 18.5, or 83.25 square inches).

You increased the wing area, so you'll have to do the same for the horizontal tail area. To find the tail area you need, divide the modified wingspan (not tailspan) by the original wingspan and multiply the result by the original tail area. In the example the modified wingspan is 61.5″ and the original wingspan is 46″. I divided 61.5 by 46 to get 1.34, then multiplied that result by the original tail area (83.25) to get 111.6 square inches. This is the area of the tail after modification.

Next subtract the original tail area from the modified area. In the example that's 111.6 − 83.3, or 28.3 square inches. This is the total area to be added to the tail, but since there are two extensions, each should be only half this area, or 14.15 square inches.

You know that the chord of the ex-

tensions has to be the same as that of the tip (4″ in the example) so you can find the length of those extensions by dividing the area of one extender panel by the chord — that is, 14.15 ÷ 4 = 3.54″. So if your plane matches the example, the tip extensions will each be rectangles 4″ by 3½″.

Now that you know the dimensions of the wing and tail extensions, you can get down to work. The wing extension may be built up from balsa, as the original wing probably was, or it can be made from foam. If you build the extensions from balsa, make them just as you did the rest of the wing. In fact, if you're working from a kit, make the extensions an integral part of the wing by simply using more ribs and longer spars. If the plane is already built, you'll have to construct the extensions separately and glue them in place.

If you use a foam core for the extensions, as I did on the Box Fly, make sure it has the same type of airfoil as the original wing. For instance, if the original airfoil is flat-bottomed, use a flat-bottomed wing core, not a symmetrical or semi-symmetrical one.

Wing cores are available from Wing Manufacturing and other suppliers that advertise in model magazines. You may be able to buy a foam core specifically designed for your airplane, which would be ideal. If not, you can use a slightly tapered core, as I did on the Box Fly, and cut it so that the forward and rear tapers are identical when the extension is installed. If you do this, the formula I gave will yield a slightly wrong answer, but it will be close enough. It's already off a bit because it assumes the extensions are weightless.

Note that the core used on the Box Fly modification is thicker than the original airfoil. This actually gives a more stable airplane, so don't worry if the extensions are a little thick. Just

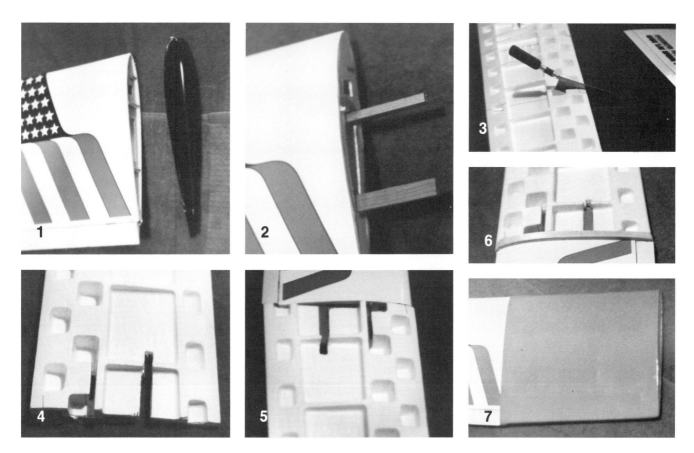

Here's how to lengthen the Box Fly's wingspan. 1. Pry off the wing tip. 2. Epoxy spruce spars in place. 3. Cut an appropriate length of foam wing core. 4. Make slots in the wing core to accept the spars. 5. Align the extension carefully and epoxy it in place. Be sure to use epoxy because most other adhesives either eat foam or don't adhere well to it. 6. Build a platform on top of the original wing using balsa strips. 7. Cover the extensions with a low-temperature heat-shrink plastic covering material such as Solarfilm. 8. After also lengthening the horizontal stabilizer, the final product should look like this.

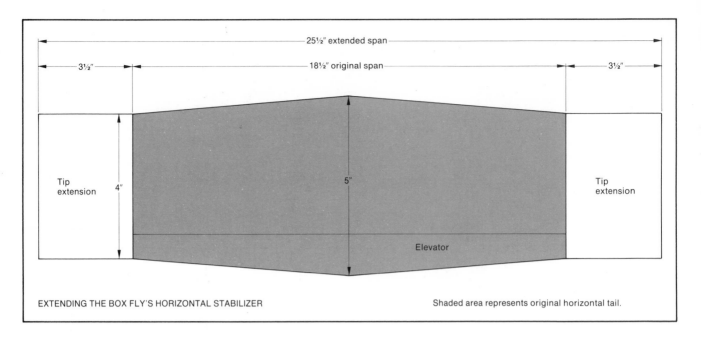

Shaded area represents original horizontal tail.

don't use extensions that are thinner than the original wing or you may get a nasty handling airplane.

Once you've gotten the wing extensions together, but not yet installed, you can turn your attention to the horizontal tail extensions. There's not much to them. In the example given, they are just a couple of balsa rectangles that match the thickness of the original stabilizer. The only special precaution is to make sure the grain runs perpendicular to the fuselage, not parallel.

You'll also notice that in modifying the Box Fly, I angled the tail extensions down about 30 degrees to add rigidity to the tail. If nothing else, it will reduce the risk of flutter. It will also invalidate the calculations for added tail area, decreasing the effective addition in the example from 34 percent to 29 percent. This is not enough to worry about. The plane flies just fine with only a 29 percent increase.

If you have a Box Fly, proceed exactly as described below. If you have some other plane, adapt the procedure to your needs.

First, pry off the plastic wing tips. Then cut four ½" x ⅜" hardwood spars about 6" long, and epoxy them into the wing as shown. Make sure they fit flush against the wooden spars already inside the wing and that they run parallel to the wing's leading edge. Use a relatively slow-curing epoxy for this operation so you have time to get everything right.

Next, find the place where the foam core is exactly as wide as the Box Fly wing (including ailerons). Cut the core at this point in such a way that when attached to the wing, it will taper the same amount from the front of the wing as from the rear. Now measure out whatever distance you calculated as the length of the extension, and cut the foam core again at that point. This is your wing extension core.

Now cut slots in the extension core as shown. These should fit snugly over the spars. Check for proper alignment before gluing the extensions in place. When you're absolutely certain the leading and trailing edges of the extensions and the leading and trailing edges of the wing can be lined up perfectly, remove the extensions and apply slow-curing epoxy to both the extensions and the spars. Next, slip the extensions over the spars, align them exactly, and pin in place. Finally, check the alignment one more time before the epoxy cures. Misalignment of an extension could make your plane unflyable, so get it right.

After the epoxy has set and the extensions are firmly in place, epoxy ⅜" x ⅟₁₆" balsa cap strips to the original wing surface, as shown. The idea is to make a platform flush with the extensions that will provide a surface for the extension covering material to grip. Build this platform layer by layer, adding as many cap strips as needed, and sand the final layer flush. Do not get epoxy on the top of the platform because it will prevent the covering material from sticking to the wing. The extensions can now be covered with a low-temperature heat-shrink material such as Solarfilm.

Now to enlarge the horizontal stabilizer. First, pry off the stab tips. Then cut out a piece of ¼" hard balsa sheet 4¼" x 5¼". Bevel the extension and round the leading and trailing edges to match those of the stab and elevator. Epoxy the extensions to the stab and pin them in place. When the epoxy cures, cover the extensions with heat-shrink film.

The modifications are complete. Before proceeding, though, check for proper alignment, balance, and control response as described in Chapter 3.

It's a good idea to have an assistant hold the plane while you start the engine.

5. The engine

Even though properly set up engines require almost no attention, you'll see people at the field who spend more time tinkering than flying. There's a moral in that observation: Set the engine up right the first time.

With minor exceptions, what I say here applies not only to the two-cycle engines that most RC pilots fly, but also to the increasingly popular four-cycles. However, since four-cycle glow engines do have a few peculiarities, I'll cover them separately later.

The main objective of this chapter is to help you get your engine running and properly tuned so that you can concentrate on learning to fly. In most cases, the general instructions that follow will be enough, but for those with balky engines, I've included a section on troubleshooting.

Engine starting and break-in procedures. If you've properly installed it, your engine should be ready to run. Fill the fuel tank and open the needle valve as many turns as the manufacturer recommends. Connect the fuel line to the carburetor and the vent line to the muffler pressure fitting. If the muffler

has no pressure fitting, install one. Turn on your radio system and open the throttle all the way. Hold the plane vertical for a couple of seconds to drain any fuel from the line, then set it down on a level spot and choke the engine by placing your left index finger over the carburetor venturi while you turn the prop through a couple of revolutions. THE GLOW PLUG CLIP SHOULD NOT BE CONNECTED WHILE YOU DO THIS.

As you choke the engine, fuel should begin to move from the tank to the carburetor. Watch the fuel line to make sure this happens. If it doesn't, open the needle valve another turn and try again. Repeat this procedure until the line fills with fuel.

Now, while an assistant holds the plane from behind, connect the battery to the glow plug and press the rotating starter cone to the prop spinner for a couple of seconds. If you don't use a starter, you'll have to flip the prop counterclockwise. Don't do this with your fingers. Use a "chicken stick."

However you decide to turn the prop, the engine may or may not start on the

first few tries. If it does, fine; if not, move on to the next approach. With the battery still connected, grasp the prop and turn it over slowly. If you feel a "bump," disconnect the fuel line and vent line and keep trying to start the engine. It will probably fire after a few tries and run very fast for a second or two as it burns up fuel that was sloshing around in the crankcase.

If it doesn't even pop, or if you didn't feel the "bump" to begin with, choke the engine and try again (with the fuel line reconnected if you disconnected it earlier). If at any point you find that you can't easily turn the engine over, it is badly flooded. Don't try to force it to turn in that condition.

Instead, remove the glow plug and gasket and use the electric starter to turn the prop for a couple of seconds. This will send a spray of fuel out of the glow plug hole, so protect your eyes when you do it. I usually just close mine, but wearing goggles is a better idea. Once you've cleared the flooding, check the plug to be sure it glows brightly and try again.

It may take a while the first time as

Close the high-speed needle valve (the one connected to the fuel line) completely, then open it the number of turns recommended by the engine manufacturer.

Choke the engine by sealing the carburetor throat with a fingertip and turning the propeller slowly by hand. To prevent accidental ignition the glow clip must not be connected.

you alternate between the engine being either flooded or dry, but before too long it should fire up, at least briefly. When it does, it may run slowly, spitting a cloud of unburned fuel from the muffler. If so, you're in luck because that's how you want it to run during the break-in period. If you are less lucky, it will behave in one of the following ways:

● It may run fast, in which case you should immediately open the needle valve to slow it down. If it doesn't slow quickly, pinch the fuel line to stop it. You don't need an overheated engine. For the same reason, do not slow it down using the throttle.

● It may run fast and quit. In this case, open the needle valve a couple of turns,

choke the engine once more, and restart.
● It may run slowly and quit. If it does this, close the needle valve a turn and restart. Do not choke the engine in this case.

● It may pop a few times and do nothing more, or it may do nothing to begin with. Either way, chances are it needs more fuel, so open the needle valve a turn, choke the engine, and try again. If you get no response to repeated attempts to start the engine after you choke it, it is probably flooded, so remove the glow plug and clear the flood with the starter as described earlier.

However, you can instead try to simply burn out the flood. To do this, disconnect the fuel line and vent line (but not the battery) and apply the starter.

After a few tries the engine may cough; keep trying and it will either quit popping because it has burned out all the fuel, or it will run briefly, gaining speed for a few seconds, and then stop abruptly when the fuel in the crankcase runs out. In either event, just reconnect the fuel line and vent line, choke the engine again, and repeat the starting procedure. If it again burns up all the fuel and doesn't run for more than a few seconds, open the needle valve another turn before your next attempt.

With patience you should be able to get the engine going. If it won't run no matter what, see the section on troubleshooting.

Once you've gotten the thing started, run it as slowly as possible for the first

If you don't have an electric starter, use a chicken stick. You can buy a chicken stick or make one from a short piece of broomstick covered with a section of rubber hose.

Hold the prop securely while feeling for a "bump."

Use the needle valve, not the throttle, to keep your new engine running slowly.

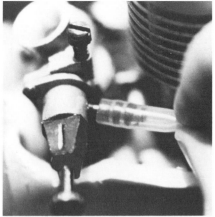

It's easy to stop the engine by pinching the fuel line with your fingers.

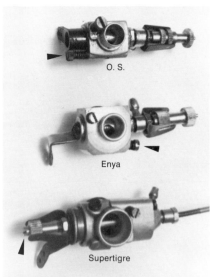

Idle adjustment screws have a confusing variety of shapes and can be hidden at various locations on the carburetor. Happily, most seldom need attention.

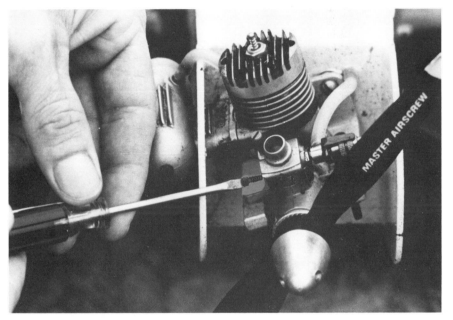

Stop the engine to adjust the idle; otherwise you risk serious injury.

few minutes. Do not close the throttle to do this. Instead, open the needle valve as far as you can without stopping the engine. In the beginning, the engine may run 30 seconds or a minute this way and then quit. This is normal for a new engine. Just restart it and continue.

After a couple of minutes of running, screw the needle valve in until the engine picks up speed, but don't let it get too fast yet. As soon as it speeds up, open the needle valve again and slow it down. Continue this procedure through the whole tank of fuel, increasing both the frequency and duration of the high-speed runs. If at any time the engine begins to sag while running fast, open the needle valve immediately to slow it down and prevent damage from overheating.

With most engines two or three tankfuls of fuel provide enough break-in to give reliable performance, but a few require much more time. To find out whether your engine is ready to fly,

close the needle valve until you reach maximum rpm, then back it out a quarter turn or so.

The engine should continue to scream without tightening up and slowing down. If it does slow down and doesn't sound rich (you'll know by this time what a rich engine sounds like) open the needle valve to a very rich setting to cool the engine, then continue the break-in procedure until it passes the test. If it holds the high speed without any problem, it's ready for you to set the idle adjustment. (By now the engine can be started with the throttle nearly closed, which greatly reduces the risk to your fingers if you flip by hand.)

For some reason many people have trouble with the idle adjustment, but if done right, it is simplicity itself. First make sure the setscrew that restricts throttle movement is adjusted so that you can close the venturi all the way. To my mind, these setscrews are useless annoyances. Unfortunately, every

RC engine I've seen has one and won't work if you remove it. Adjust it so you can fully close the venturi, then forget it.

Having taken care of the setscrew, open the throttle all the way and adjust for maximum rpm with the high-speed needle valve. Then back off about a quarter turn so the engine doesn't run too lean, and with the throttle trim lever set as high as it will go, close the throttle stick all the way. If you are lucky, you will be able both to set the idle exactly where you want it with the trim lever and to shut the engine off by moving the trim all the way down.

If you're less lucky, the engine will either turn over too fast with the trim lever fully closed or, when you fully close the throttle, will quit with the trim fully open. If the engine turns over too fast at idle, you'll have to adjust the throttle linkage so that you can actually turn it off with the trim lever. The hard part is that you still need a fully open carburetor when the throttle is wide open. Meeting both conditions usually requires adjusting both the servo and throttle arms to get the right throw; some radio systems allow you to make the adjustment electronically.

However your engine responded when you idled it, the next step is to try to improve that response. To do this, first open the throttle full bore, then close it and use the trim tab to idle the engine as slowly as possible. After about ten seconds of slow idling, open the throttle as fast as you can. Most likely, the engine will sputter or even quit when you do this. If it doesn't quit, shut it down and adjust the low-speed idle setting. Most engines have either a setscrew or a second needle valve for adjusting the idle. Turn this adjustment a quarter turn in one direction. It doesn't matter which direction you first turn it.

The four-cycle engine looks, sounds, and behaves just a little different.

Removing the valve cover on this O.S. four-cycle engine reveals the rocker arms, springs, and adjustment screws.

These are the sort of tools supplied with a four-cycle engine. Use them sparingly.

Some people adjust the idle with the engine running. This is asking to have a screwdriver thrown into your face. FIRST STOP THE ENGINE, THEN ADJUST THE IDLE.

Now get the engine going again, open it wide until it reaches peak rpm, then close the throttle and use the trim to set the idle as slow as you can. Wait about ten seconds and then open the throttle as fast as possible. If the engine takes longer to quit than the first time, or if it sputters less, you're on the right track. Shut it down, move the adjustment another quarter turn in the same direction, and repeat the procedure. If the engine sounds worse, turn the adjustment the other way.

Continue this process until you pass the optimum adjustment point. Then back up in eighth turns to get the best possible idle setting. At this point, when you open the throttle from idle, there should be almost no hesitation as the engine moves from slow speed to full power.

You're not quite done yet. Your adjustments to the low-speed needle may have affected the high-speed setting and vice versa. Make the necessary adjustments to the high-speed needle, then correct the low-speed again. Usually once is enough, but if you have to reset both needles several times, it won't take long, and it will be worth it. Once the low-speed needle is properly set, you will rarely have to touch it.

Four-cycle glow-ignition engines.
In the past couple of years the four-cy-cle engine has begun to chip away at the dominance long held by the two-cy-cle glow engine. It is quieter and sounds more like a full-size airplane engine. You operate it almost exactly like a two-cycle engine, but there are a few differences.

First, four-cycles like to start wet. They can be choked into this condition, but since the carburetor is often out of reach, they are usually primed through the exhaust ports (they don't normally use mufflers). Second, like other engines, they develop hydraulic lock if you get them too wet, and this is a frequent occurrence, so be on the lookout for it.

The four-cycle also has a reputation for vicious backfiring, which I believe, having nearly lost a fingertip while flipping a small one barehanded. No need for you to be that stupid — use a starter motor, or at least a chicken stick.

Unlike the standard two-cycle engine, the four-stroker has adjustable valves and comes with a set of gauges and wrenches to adjust them. If you have to, go ahead and adjust the valves per the manufacturer's instructions, but don't do so just for kicks. The adjustments are easy to foul up and it may take you a long time to get the engine running right again.

Remember that glow plug without the idle bar I told you to get rid of? Here's the place to use it. Four-strokers don't need idle bars. If you have idle problems and are using low-nitro fuel,

move up to a blend that contains 15 percent nitromethane. If that doesn't work, try one of the special four-cycle plugs or rig up a battery to heat the plug at low idle settings — but not the battery that powers your servos and receiver.

The four-cycle engine likes to run a little rich, and unlike the two-cycle, won't give more power if you run it as lean as possible. Let it run rich and your engine will last longer.

Outside of these differences, the four-cycle engine behaves much like any other glow engine, and once you get it set up, will be so reliable you'll rarely have to touch it.

Troubleshooting. The glow engine is a simple piece of machinery that usually runs well, but occasionally a beginner (and sometimes an expert) will waste hours fooling with a balky engine. This section is intended to help you deal quickly with such machines. If your engine balks, start through the following list.

1. If the engine refuses to run, or if it runs erratically, or especially if it conks out when you remove the glow plug clip, start with the quick fixes. First, change the glow plug and check to be sure the needle valve is not free to rotate at random from engine vibration. If the problem persists try some new fuel. Improperly stored fuel can degrade quickly.

2. If you can't draw fuel by choking the engine, or if it consistently just burns the prime and stops, or if it will

Blow air into the tank through what you think is the fuel line; vent and fuel lines are reversed if fuel flows into the muffler.

A burst of air will sometimes clear an obstructed carburetor.

only run fast, no matter how far you open the needle valve, here's how to proceed:

A. Tighten all screws, bolts, and nuts on the engine, including those that hold the muffler in place. Be firm but gentle. You don't want to strip any threads.

B. Close the low-speed adjustment a turn or so and try running the engine again. If necessary, repeat until the engine runs properly or the adjustment is fully closed.

C. If you are not already using muffler pressure, run a line from the fuel tank vent to the muffler pressure fitting. This greatly improves fuel draw.

D. Check the fuel line and the muffler pressure line to be sure that: a) They are free of kinks and do not touch the engine except at the points of attachment. An innocent-looking kink, even if it doesn't completely prevent fuel draw, can make proper adjustment impossible, as can the vibration caused by contact of the fuel line with the crankcase or cylinder. b) Both lines fit tightly. Loose lines allow the engine to

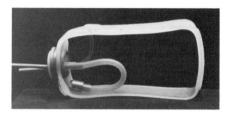

Occasionally, the clunk gets hung up in the front of the tank. Just shake the plane violently to free the clunk.

suck air, thereby reducing fuel flow. When in doubt, use the next smaller diameter line. c) The lines are not damaged. Some pinholes and slits are so hard to detect that I usually just replace the lines if I have fuel flow problems.

E. It's possible that the vent line is hooked to the carburetor and the fuel line is hooked to the muffler, the opposite of what you want. To check this, blow into what you believe to be the fuel line (the one that feeds the carburetor). Use a syringe for this operation and protect your eyes from any fuel

spray. With the tank half full and the plane level, this procedure will blow bubbles in the tank, and all that will come out the other line will be air (and maybe a drop or two of fuel). However, if you have the lines backwards, you will get a steady stream of fuel when you apply air pressure. If this happens, reverse lines.

F. If the lines are properly connected and the engine still won't work right, take your syringe and blow air through the carburetor. Now try the engine again. If it still doesn't draw fuel properly, remove the carburetor, disassemble it, and clean it with alcohol or fuel. Replace it and try again.

G. Occasionally, the clunk inside the tank gets hung up. This usually results from a rough landing, so it shouldn't be a problem with your new airplane. But if all else fails, check to be sure. If the clunk is hung up, shake the tank (or the whole airplane) until it comes free.

Almost certainly your engine will be running properly before you get to the end of this list. If it's not, consult the club expert or contact the manufacturer.

When adjusting or testing a running engine, use your legs to prevent the plane from moving. This pilot would be well-advised to use a neck strap.

6. Ground handling

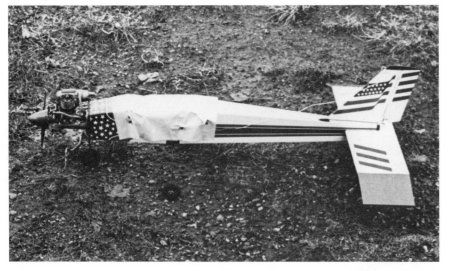

This chapter is about ground handling, and just to make sure about the ground part, the first thing to do is remove the plane's wings. Tape paper or Saran Wrap over the wing saddle to keep oil out of the fuselage. As an added precaution, take about ten feet of heavy twine, tie one end securely around the fuselage just forward of the tail, and make a loop for your right hand in the other end. You now have a safety harness to stop the plane by force if you suddenly forget how to use the throttle stick.

Having completed these safety preparations, find a deserted parking lot or field where you can practice in solitude. You won't have great control of the plane at first, and if there are people around, you could easily run into one of them. Also, when choosing the field, remember that there are no brakes on your plane, so stay away from hills. If you're using an asphalt or concrete field, even a tiny rise can be treacherous.

The harness looks silly, but has prevented an accident or two and once saved a terrified dog from a propeller. Use it till you get a feel for taxiing. Here's how to get started.

Range check the radio. If you have an assistant, you can do this with the engine running, which is the best way. Otherwise, leave the engine turned off. To perform the range test, turn on your receiver and transmitter. With the antenna on the transmitter collapsed, walk away from the plane until you have reached the distance specified by the manufacturer or until you lose radio control. If the radio quits before you get to the specified distance, don't operate the plane, even on the ground, until the problem is corrected.

Lay the harness out behind the plane. Start the engine, set it to idle, and check to make sure the plane won't move when you release it. On pavement this requires a slow idle.

Pick up the transmitter and straddle the fuselage ahead of the horizontal stabilizer with your legs to prevent the plane from moving.

Open the engine full bore to be sure it's running right, then return it to idle, and check one last time to be sure the plane will not move when you release it.

Make sure your transmitter is solidly attached to your body by the neck strap. You can't do this exercise safely without a neck strap.

Step behind the plane, pick up the loop in the harness, hold it firmly in your right hand, and take up the slack so the plane can't get a running start.

Without wings, the modified Box Fly looks like a giant larval insect or creature from a bad dream. Looks aren't what counts, though. Your first objective is to keep the plane on the ground.

Slowly open the throttle until the plane begins to move, and then shut it down immediately. Try again, this time finding a setting that makes the plane move at a comfortable walking speed. If you're on grass, you'll probably have to alternately open and close the throttle in short bursts to maintain a more or less constant speed.

Follow the plane around for a while, getting a feel for the steering and throttle controls. After you've run a couple of tankfuls of fuel through this way and feel confident that if anything goes wrong you will instinctively chop the throttle, remove and discard the harness. You've completed the first step in learning to fly RC.

Next, try following the plane around a bit without the harness. Then you can try standing in one place and steering the plane in circles and figure eights in front of you. After you're comfortable with that, try sending the plane out and back along a straight line.

You will quickly realize that when the plane is coming toward you it seems to steer backwards. Just take it easy and with practice steering will become automatic regardless of which direction you're going. Until that happens, though, be especially careful. The plane can accelerate to 40 or 50 mph faster than you'd imagine, so be prepared first to chop the throttle in an emergency, and second, to apply rudder control if the plane is headed toward you or anyone else. Either left or right rudder will save your skin, but program yourself ahead of time to give one or the other if trouble develops. Don't sit there debating which way to turn while the plane runs you down.

Once you've gotten the circles and figure eights and the out-and-back sorties down pat, make an obstacle course, and while you stand in one spot, run the plane through the course several times in both directions. It's more difficult than it sounds, but like everything else in RC, it gets easier with practice. Just don't get so involved in steering that you forget to cut the throttle if the plane moves too fast.

Having mastered the obstacle course with your flightless fuselage, put the wings on and try it again. The plane will handle a little differently now, and if there's a bit of wind, it may be even harder to steer. It may even tip over, which is an annoyance but not a serious problem. The real danger is that if the plane gets too much speed, it will become airborne, a bad idea because you don't know how to fly it yet. Keep the speed down and practice till you're good and bored.

Then take the plane home, and while the batteries are charging, read the next few chapters of this book so you'll better appreciate what the airplane does when you finally see it in the sky.

The leash looks silly, but just about guarantees you won't hurt anybody.

After mastering the throttle, let the plane run free while you practice steering.

Install the wings and keep practicing but don't let the plane become airborne.

When flying an F-15 (or in this case, an L-19) the pilot of a full-size plane sees ground, not airplane. Under the best of circumstances, the RC pilot sees an airplane, not the ground.

7. The basics of RC flight

Your first memories of flying RC will probably go something like this: You've just tried your first turn with that brand-new airplane and now you can see it — 200 feet up and headed toward earth in a 100-mile-an-hour death spiral. Your right hand reflexively holds the stick as far back as it will go (which is what got you into this mess) and you wait for the impact. Vaguely you hear a voice say, "I've got it," and watch the plane level out and climb back upstairs as if nothing out of the ordinary had happened.

In fact, what happened was very ordinary for a first RC flight. When you lost it, the instructor took over on the buddy box and saved your plane. On a conscious level you may know all there

is to know about flying RC, but the instructor can react appropriately without thinking, and you can't. It's demoralizing to a novice to be so helpless, but we all have to go through this phase before we can fly RC; and I mean everybody — even pilots of full-size planes.

A few years ago, a stranger appeared at our club field, approached a group of RC fliers, and announced that he was an ex-fighter pilot looking for the hottest combination of RC airplane and engine on the market. No trainers for him. No instructor, either. I wasn't in the group he spoke to, but I overheard and felt embarrassed for the man because, as luck would have it, all three of the RC fliers he'd cornered were retired military pilots. As gently as possi-

ble, they told him that if he started flying RC, he'd start from scratch, just about even with the high school kid who didn't know an airfoil from an altimeter. "It's different," one of them said. "I flew jets for 20 years and had to learn all over when I got into this hobby."

The newcomer wasn't listening, or at least he wasn't believing. He knew he could fly anything with wings, and since the argument wasn't changing his mind, I walked over and invited him to fly my Chickenship, an aerobatic home-brew airplane. When he accepted the offer, I hooked up the buddy box and took the plane to about 300 feet before switching control over to him.

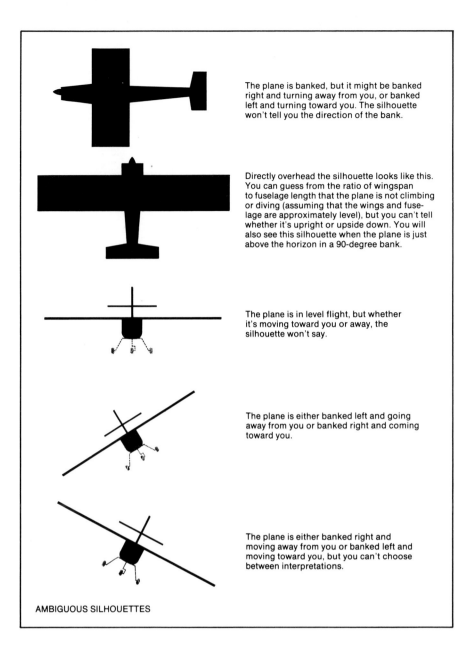

The plane is banked, but it might be banked right and turning away from you, or banked left and turning toward you. The silhouette won't tell you the direction of the bank.

Directly overhead the silhouette looks like this. You can guess from the ratio of wingspan to fuselage length that the plane is not climbing or diving (assuming that the wings and fuselage are approximately level), but you can't tell whether it's upright or upside down. You will also see this silhouette when the plane is just above the horizon in a 90-degree bank.

The plane is in level flight, but whether it's moving toward you or away, the silhouette won't say.

The plane is either banked left and going away from you or banked right and coming toward you.

The plane is either banked right and moving away from you or banked left and moving toward you, but you can't choose between interpretations.

AMBIGUOUS SILHOUETTES

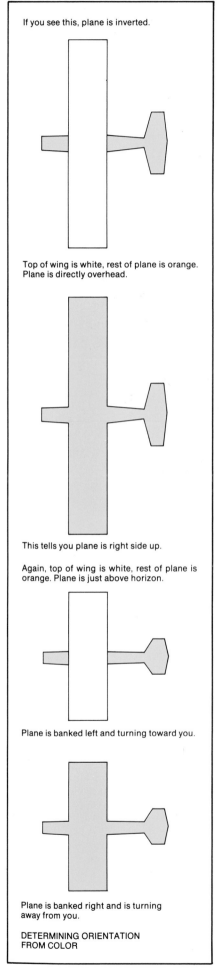

If you see this, plane is inverted.

Top of wing is white, rest of plane is orange. Plane is directly overhead.

This tells you plane is right side up.

Again, top of wing is white, rest of plane is orange. Plane is just above horizon.

Plane is banked left and turning toward you.

Plane is banked right and is turning away from you.

DETERMINING ORIENTATION FROM COLOR

Five seconds later, the Chickenship was in a spiral dive and my new student was complaining that it didn't fly like a real plane. I pulled it out, climbed back to altitude, and gave it to him again, along with some instructions on turning. Instantly, he put it into a series of unintentional loops and rolls and again ended in a spiral dive. After half a dozen tries, he managed only one 90-degree turn without losing it. I landed then and he sheepishly agreed that he wasn't ready for a hot RC plane and that the lesson had saved him several hundred dollars and lots of building time.

His initial overconfidence was understandable. After all, RC planes fly on the same principles as the jet fighters he was at home with. The problem was that he'd flown from inside the cockpit, relying on cues that in no way resembled the ones RC pilots use. Not only did he not see the same things, he had no instruments to help him, and the seat-of-the-pants feel of full-size

planes was absent. If he'd had time to mull things over, he could have figured out what to do, but RC flying only gives enough time for reflexes, not deliberate thought, and his brain, accustomed to dealing with one set of inputs, could not instantly adjust to new ones.

The purpose of this chapter is to lay down the basics — the things you have to reduce to instinct if you're going to fly RC. It begins with the visual cues that so befuddled the old fighter jock.

Interpreting silhouettes. The average spectator, even though he's watching the same airplane as the RC pilot who's flying it, doesn't see quite the same things. And what does the pilot see? An airplane, of course, but only some of the time. Just as often he's looking at the silhouette of an airplane, aware, as the onlooker is not, that silhouettes are ambiguous.

For example, the silhouette of a banked plane looks the same in certain parts of the turn whether the bank is to the left or the right, and the silhouette

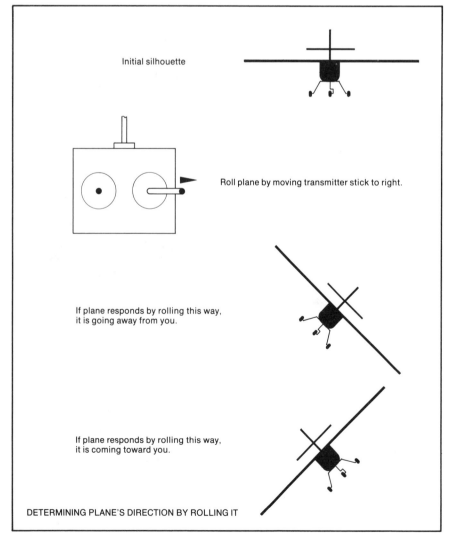

Initial silhouette

Roll plane by moving transmitter stick to right.

If plane responds by rolling this way, it is going away from you.

If plane responds by rolling this way, it is coming toward you.

DETERMINING PLANE'S DIRECTION BY ROLLING IT

of a plane nearly overhead looks the same whether the plane is right side up or inverted.

I once saw a top scale pilot crash because he thought his plane was inverted when it was right side up. It was just a silhouette against a gray sky, and having made the initial mistake, he wasn't able to regain perspective before his plane plowed a 30-foot furrow full of balsa scraps across the field. Because it was a military scale airplane, his model had to be olive drab all around, like the original. If it had been a sport plane, and if the top of the wing had been orange and the bottom green, he probably would not have made his first mistake because the wing would have shown enough color to tell him which side was up. Even if it had initially appeared as a silhouette, he would have seen flashes of color as the plane dived and rolled, and this would have allowed him to reorient himself and regain control.

Color also gives useful information when turning. If you see the color of the top of the wing, you know the plane is banked toward you. If you see the color of the underside, it is banked away.

Because a flash of color from the wing tells the pilot which end is up and which way the plane is banked — provided top and bottom don't look the same — RC fliers have a rule of thumb: Paint the top and bottom of the wing different colors. Bright reds and oranges are the most visible. Don't use dark shades. White alone is not good because it blends into the sky. Black,

Even when a radio control model flies straight, the pilot's view of it keeps changing. This Cessna 152 is not turning between frames, but as it moves farther away from the pilot, he sees less of the side and relatively more of its wingspan. Notice also that the farther out the plane gets, the more it looks like an indistinct gray silhouette.

which is always seen as a silhouette, should be avoided.

In poor lighting, or at great distance, even bright colors look like silhouettes, and when you're not sure of the plane's orientation, the only way to find out where it's headed is to give it a command and interpret the resultant movement. Suppose, for instance, that your plane has strayed off too far and is now just a thin, dark horizontal line moving away from you. Or is it coming toward you? The silhouette won't tell. The experienced pilot rarely gets into this fix because he doesn't let the plane get that far from him, and his plane goes where he points it, so even though the silhouette offers no clue, he knows where it's headed.

On the rare occasion when he does get confused, he has an easy way of sorting things out. He just banks his plane steeply to see which way it rolls. If he moves the stick to the right and the plane rolls to the right, then he knows it is moving away from him. If it rolls left, it is coming toward him.

If the plane is far out and low, a similar technique can tell you whether it is banked toward or away from you. First try to level the wings by rolling in one direction. Say you roll to the right. If the plane is steeply banked to its left, the wings will move toward level and you will see a smaller wing silhouette. If the wing silhouette gets much larger, you were already banked right and will have to reverse the stick and roll left to level the plane. Unfortunately, this technique will not work if the plane is

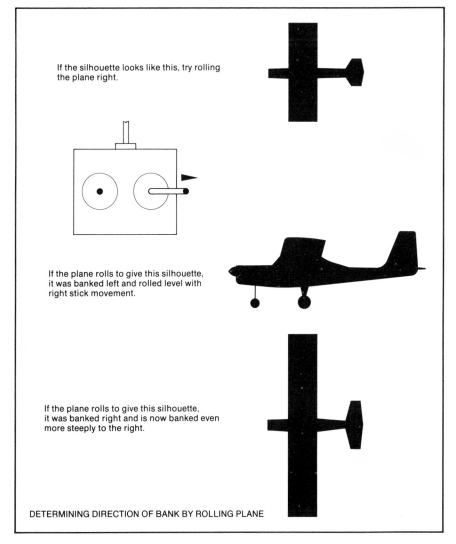

If the silhouette looks like this, try rolling the plane right.

If the plane rolls to give this silhouette, it was banked left and rolled level with right stick movement.

If the plane rolls to give this silhouette, it was banked right and is now banked even more steeply to the right.

DETERMINING DIRECTION OF BANK BY ROLLING PLANE

If plane is far away, you may see only an indistinct silhouette like this . . .

To determine whether it is upright or inverted, apply down elevator on transmitter stick.

If the plane is inverted, it will climb and look like this . . .

If the plane is upright, it will dive and look like this . . .

If plane is nearly overhead, its silhouette will look like this . . .

To determine whether it is upright or inverted, give down elevator.

If plane is inverted, you may see very little effect, although it will be climbing.

If plane is upright, it will dive toward the ground and very quickly get closer to you. Once you can see it clearly, use up elevator to level out.

DETERMINING WHETHER PLANE IS UPRIGHT OR INVERTED

far above the horizon, but the technique is useful when you need it most, when the plane is low and far away.

It is possible, especially if the plane is already steeply banked when you begin this test, to end up with the wings level and the plane upside down. If you suspect this has happened, feed in some down elevator. If the plane really is inverted, it will climb, or if it has a flat-bottom airfoil, it will at least not dive steeply. In this case you can simply roll the craft upright. If the plane is not inverted to begin with, it will dive when you give down elevator and your normal instincts will cause you to give up elevator until the nose is level again.

If my friend with the scale plane had sorted things out this way, he could have saved his aircraft, but apparently he hadn't reduced those responses to instinct and didn't have time to think his way through the problem.

Because reading silhouettes is more difficult than reading about them, and because you have to respond reflexively, you won't be able to just finish this chapter and go out and do all these things fast enough to save your plane. That takes practice.

Fortunately, there is a nondestructive way to get your earliest practice. Visit the local flying field and watch other pilots' planes in the air. Try to follow them through maneuvers and guess whether they're banked left or right, and whether they're right side up or inverted. You'll be surprised how often you guess wrong. In the beginning it's almost as instructive as really flying — and it's free.

How airplanes fly and maneuver. So far, when I've explained how to orient yourself, I've spoken as if you knew exactly how to move the controls, which, except for those of you who are pilots of full-size planes, isn't true. Now it's time to tackle that task and explain how airplanes fly and maneuver.

We all know that the wing generates lift. The Bernoulli effect explains this for a physicist, but for our purposes, it's enough to know a definition and three facts. First the definition: The angle of attack is the angle of the wing relative to the airflow. It only occasionally coincides with the angle the wing makes with the horizon. The sketches explain it better than words.

Now for the facts:
• The faster the plane moves through the air, the more lift the wing develops at a given angle of attack.
• Within limits, the greater the angle of attack, the greater the lift at a given speed.
• If the angle of attack becomes too great, the wing suddenly loses lift and is said to be stalled. When this happens, the plane drops, regardless of what the pilot does with the controls.

The practical implication of all this is that to get a plane into the air, all you need to do is angle the wing properly into the airstream, which the landing gear will probably do on your trainer, and open the throttle. But to keep the plane aloft once it breaks ground, and to keep it in sight, you have to make adjustments to the four controls via your transmitter sticks. One of these sticks, as you already know, controls power; more about that later. The other three channels are used to move control surfaces which each rotate the plane about one or more of its axes.

Ideally, the elevator controls pitch. Up elevator points the nose up and down elevator points it down.

Rudder controls yaw. If you move the rudder stick on your transmitter to the left, the ideal plane will simply cock its nose to the left, but continue to fly the same straight and level path as before. Some aerobatic planes behave this way, but because your trainer has a high wing with generous dihedral, it responds in a more complicated way. It will yaw when you apply rudder, but the yaw makes it aerodynamically unstable with respect to pitch and roll, which leads the plane to roll in the direction of the yaw and to pitch its nose down. The result is a downward turn.

The ailerons cause your plane to roll. On some models, they also cause a serious yaw in the direction opposite the roll, which requires rudder correction. That's not a problem on a well-set-up trainer, except at low speeds, and for present purposes, we can act as if ailerons do nothing but roll the airplane.

Now that we've figured out all the individual controls, we need to put them together to make the plane do what we want. The first thing you will have to do when your instructor hands you the controls is keep the wings level. With a trainer, you do this using either rudder or aileron, whichever is on the right stick. If the plane is going away from you, your instincts will probably tell you to level the wings by pushing the right stick in the direction of the high wing, which is the correct way to do it. Just gently move the stick in that direction until the high wing comes even with the low one, and then return the stick to neutral.

If the plane is coming toward you, you'll feel like you're trying to fly in a mirror because the plane's left is to your right and its right is to your left. At first everyone is confused by this, but take heart. You learned to comb your hair, which requires the same kind of mental turnaround, and you'll learn to fly RC. Until you get used to flying toward yourself, though, drill one rule into your head until it is pure reflex. IF THE PLANE IS HEADED TOWARD YOU WITH ONE WING LOW, MOVE THE RIGHT STICK IN THE DIRECTION OF THE LOW WING. This rule has saved many a beginner's

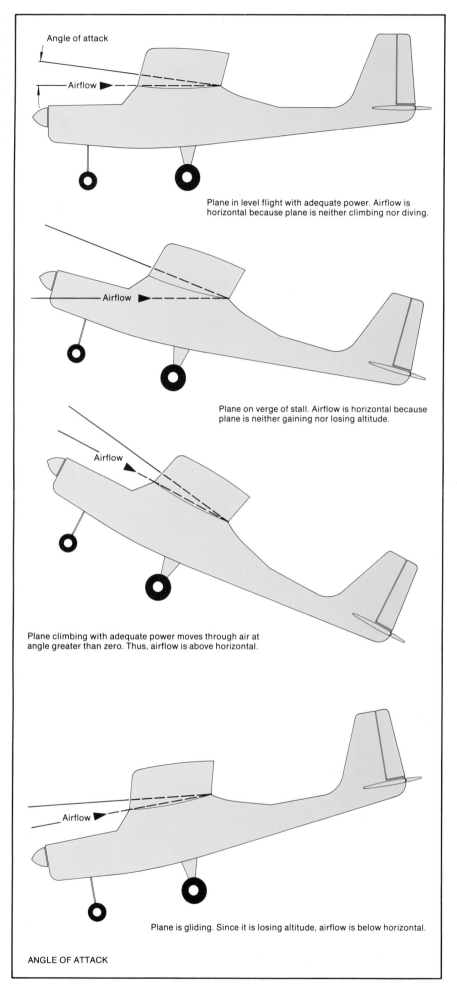

Angle of attack

Airflow

Plane in level flight with adequate power. Airflow is horizontal because plane is neither climbing nor diving.

Airflow

Plane on verge of stall. Airflow is horizontal because plane is neither gaining nor losing altitude.

Airflow

Plane climbing with adequate power moves through air at angle greater than zero. Thus, airflow is above horizontal.

Airflow

Plane is gliding. Since it is losing altitude, airflow is below horizontal.

ANGLE OF ATTACK

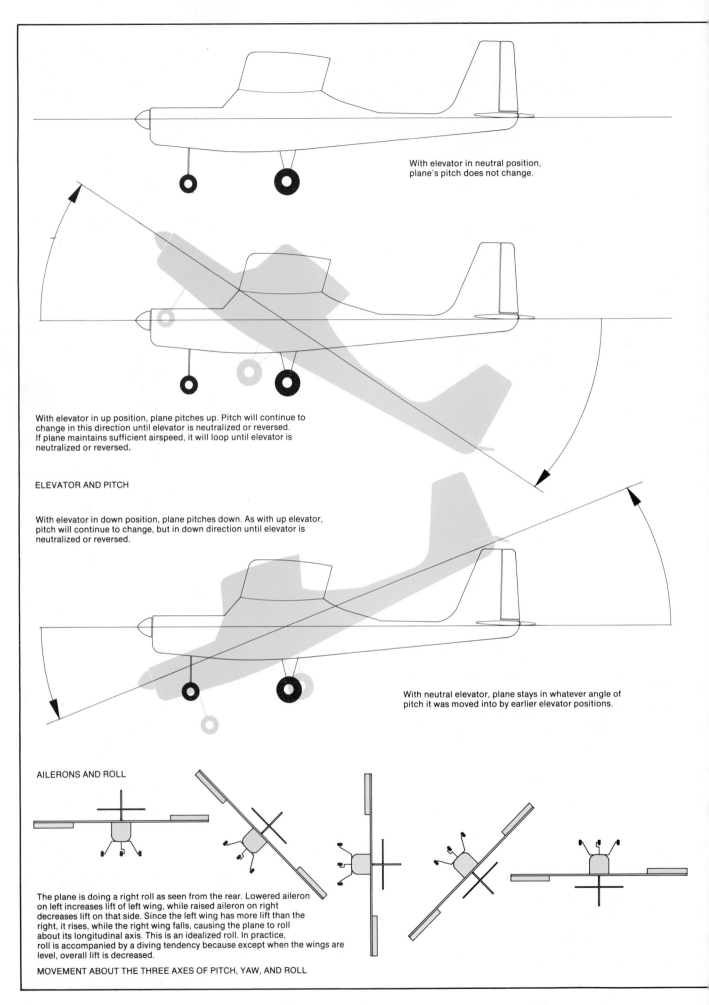

With elevator in neutral position, plane's pitch does not change.

With elevator in up position, plane pitches up. Pitch will continue to change in this direction until elevator is neutralized or reversed. If plane maintains sufficient airspeed, it will loop until elevator is neutralized or reversed.

ELEVATOR AND PITCH

With elevator in down position, plane pitches down. As with up elevator, pitch will continue to change, but in down direction until elevator is neutralized or reversed.

With neutral elevator, plane stays in whatever angle of pitch it was moved into by earlier elevator positions.

AILERONS AND ROLL

The plane is doing a right roll as seen from the rear. Lowered aileron on left increases lift of left wing, while raised aileron on right decreases lift on that side. Since the left wing has more lift than the right, it rises, while the right wing falls, causing the plane to roll about its longitudinal axis. This is an idealized roll. In practice, roll is accompanied by a diving tendency because except when the wings are level, overall lift is decreased.

MOVEMENT ABOUT THE THREE AXES OF PITCH, YAW, AND ROLL

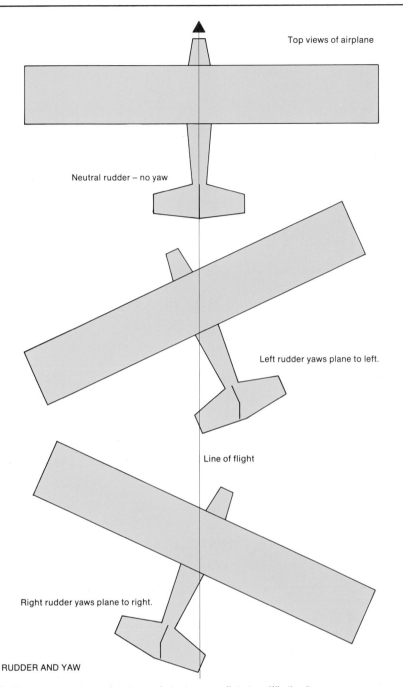

Top views of airplane

Neutral rudder – no yaw

Left rudder yaws plane to left.

Line of flight

Right rudder yaws plane to right.

RUDDER AND YAW

Rudder movement causes plane to yaw, but not necessarily to turn. Whether it turns at all, and if so, which way, depends on design factors such as wing position and dihedral. It is even possible to design a plane to turn in the direction opposite of rudder movement. Aerobatic planes yaw in response to rudder, but do not change flight direction.

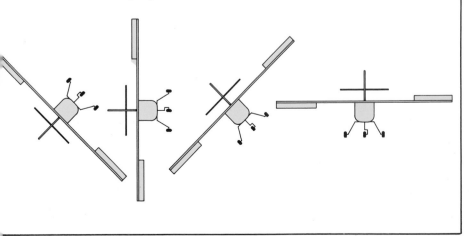

plane. Finally, on this and other control movements, remember — just a little movement on the stick until you see what happens. Don't overcontrol. Take it calmly and slowly and be prepared to reverse yourself if you guessed wrong.

Turning the plane. You can only fly an RC plane straight and level for a few seconds at a time because even a throttled-back trainer will zip out of sight at 50 mph. So the second thing you have to learn is how to turn the airplane to keep it in the area. It's easy when you get the hang of it, yet turns are where beginners usually have their first serious trouble, because turning requires that you think of several things at once.

You have to evaluate the pitch and roll of the plane from a constantly changing perspective and use that information to guide your hands as they move the right stick up and down and left to right, all at the same time. Don't despair if you lose it several times before you become comfortable with turning. Everybody has trouble at first, and everybody who keeps at it learns before long.

Here's how it's done: First you use ailerons or rudder to roll in the direction of the intended turn. You want a moderate angle of bank, not a steep one, so roll until the wings make an angle of 30 degrees or so with the horizon, then move the right stick back toward the center until the angle of bank is steady. You'll have to move the stick back and forth to maintain bank, but do so gently, smoothly, and slowly.

As we saw earlier, if you simply roll a trainer, its nose will drop. So while you're still adjusting the angle of bank, you also have to feed in enough up elevator to push the nose back up level with the horizon so that your plane doesn't dive toward the ground.

At this point many beginners make their first mistakes. As soon as they think about giving up elevator, they forget about controlling the bank and fail to neutralize the rudder or ailerons they've used to roll the plane into that bank. Typically the bank gets too steep while they're not watching it, and no matter how much up elevator they feed in, the plane loses altitude. It also turns tightly because as the bank gets steeper, the elevator acts more like a rudder.

Occasionally the bank continues until the plane rolls over on its back, at which point up elevator makes it go down in a tight spiral, unless the roll is neutralized. Even if the plane doesn't roll inverted, it will scream toward the ground in a spiral dive if the bank is too steep.

There are two lessons here. First, even when you're giving up elevator to control pitch, keep thinking about the roll so you don't overdo it. Second, if

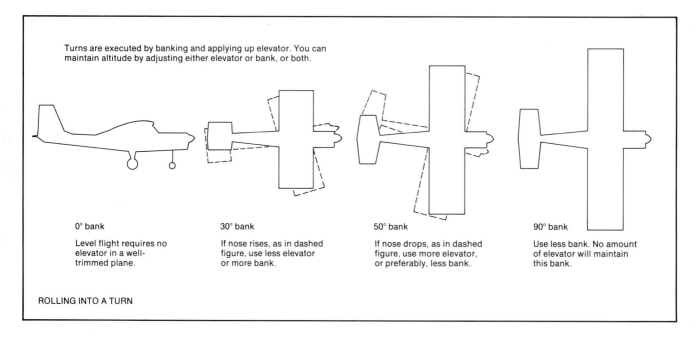

Turns are executed by banking and applying up elevator. You can maintain altitude by adjusting either elevator or bank, or both.

0° bank	30° bank	50° bank	90° bank
Level flight requires no elevator in a well-trimmed plane.	If nose rises, as in dashed figure, use less elevator or more bank.	If nose drops, as in dashed figure, use more elevator, or preferably, less bank.	Use less bank. No amount of elevator will maintain this bank.

ROLLING INTO A TURN

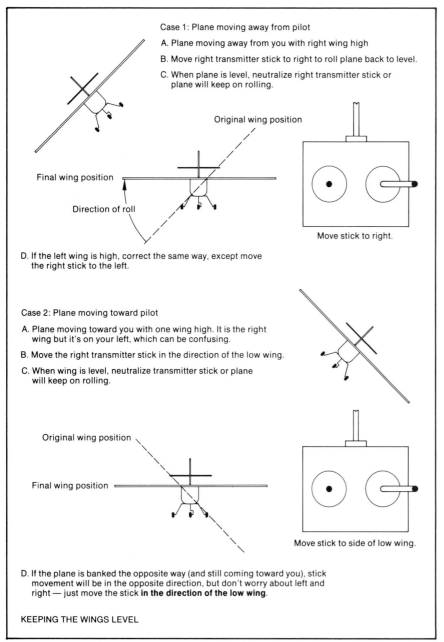

Case 1: Plane moving away from pilot

A. Plane moving away from you with right wing high

B. Move right transmitter stick to right to roll plane back to level.

C. When plane is level, neutralize right transmitter stick or plane will keep on rolling.

Original wing position

Final wing position

Direction of roll

Move stick to right.

D. If the left wing is high, correct the same way, except move the right stick to the left.

Case 2: Plane moving toward pilot

A. Plane moving toward you with one wing high. It is the right wing but it's on your left, which can be confusing.

B. Move the right transmitter stick in the direction of the low wing.

C. When wing is level, neutralize transmitter stick or plane will keep on rolling.

Original wing position

Final wing position

Move stick to side of low wing.

D. If the plane is banked the opposite way (and still coming toward you), stick movement will be in the opposite direction, but don't worry about left and right — just move the stick **in the direction of the low wing.**

KEEPING THE WINGS LEVEL

you find that no amount of up elevator will maintain altitude, move the right stick away from the turn, without touching the elevator, until the nose comes back up.

If your elevator won't hold altitude in an 80-degree bank, roll to 45 degrees and it will. In fact, at the lower angle of bank you will probably have to ease off the up elevator a bit to keep the nose down and prevent the plane from climbing. With practice, you'll learn to do all this automatically, but in the beginning, it will be a little dicey, which is why you have an instructor.

Once you've found the right combination of pitch and roll and hold your control stick steady, the plane will fly in circles until you change control settings. To come out of the turn, wait until the plane is headed where you want it to go, roll it back to level flight with the right stick, then neutralize both elevator and aileron or rudder, depending on which you used to get into the turn, and make small adjustments to maintain level flight.

Gaining and losing altitude. So far I've talked mostly about maintaining altitude, but obviously, if you're going to fly, you have to climb and descend. A good RC plane has so much wing area and power for its weight that it can climb like a full-size plane can't. Some of the real monsters will climb straight up at 40 miles an hour, and any old trainer will swoop out of the sky at 100 or more. Some people fly like that all the time except for landings. They take off under full power and leave the throttle wide open, steering the plane up and down with the elevator. You couldn't do that in a full-size airplane, but you can on a model, and if that makes you happy, go ahead. Be advised, though, that you have much more time to respond on the sticks if you throttle back to a gentle cruise and

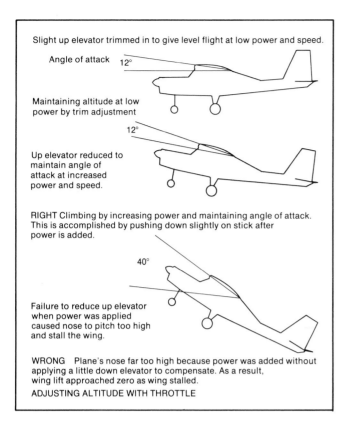

Slight up elevator trimmed in to give level flight at low power and speed.

Angle of attack   12°

Maintaining altitude at low power by trim adjustment

12°

Up elevator reduced to maintain angle of attack at increased power and speed.

RIGHT Climbing by increasing power and maintaining angle of attack. This is accomplished by pushing down slightly on stick after power is added.

40°

Failure to reduce up elevator when power was applied caused nose to pitch too high and stall the wing.

WRONG   Plane's nose far too high because power was added without applying a little down elevator to compensate. As a result, wing lift approached zero as wing stalled.

ADJUSTING ALTITUDE WITH THROTTLE

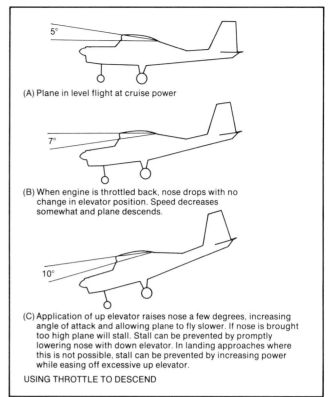

5°

(A) Plane in level flight at cruise power

7°

(B) When engine is throttled back, nose drops with no change in elevator position. Speed decreases somewhat and plane descends.

10°

(C) Application of up elevator raises nose a few degrees, increasing angle of attack and allowing plane to fly slower. If nose is brought too high plane will stall. Stall can be prevented by promptly lowering nose with down elevator. In landing approaches where this is not possible, stall can be prevented by increasing power while easing off excessive up elevator.

USING THROTTLE TO DESCEND

control altitude with throttle, rather than elevator.

If your instructor has trimmed your plane to fly hands-off without gaining or losing altitude, you can make it climb by opening the throttle a notch or two. No need to give up elevator because the plane will climb on its own as the engine speeds up. In fact, if you suddenly apply full power, you will

have to use some down elevator to keep the nose from rising too high and causing a stall.

This upward pitch in response to a power increase is characteristic of planes in which the engine is lower than the wing, and leads to the paradox that sometimes you have to give down elevator to go up. Don't be afraid to push the nose firmly back toward the hori-

zon if it gets too high; just do so smoothly and slowly and don't let it drop into a dive.

Conversely, if you start at half throttle in level flight and you want to bring the plane lower, just chop throttle and the plane will drop its nose and descend. If it starts to gain speed, slow it down with a little up elevator. Again, the paradox — you can use up elevator

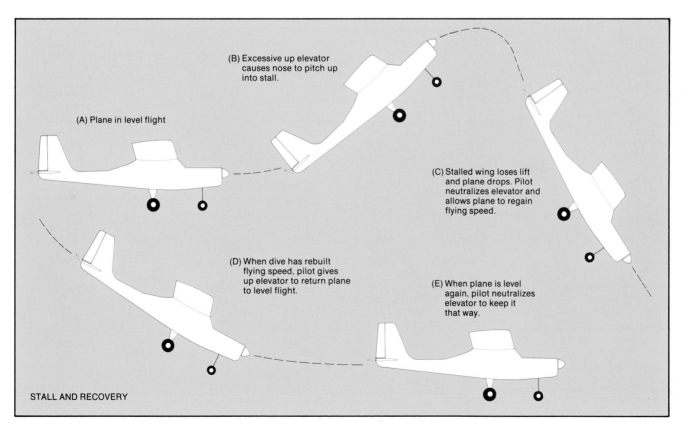

(B) Excessive up elevator causes nose to pitch up into stall.

(A) Plane in level flight

(C) Stalled wing loses lift and plane drops. Pilot neutralizes elevator and allows plane to regain flying speed.

(D) When dive has rebuilt flying speed, pilot gives up elevator to return plane to level flight.

(E) When plane is level again, pilot neutralizes elevator to keep it that way.

STALL AND RECOVERY

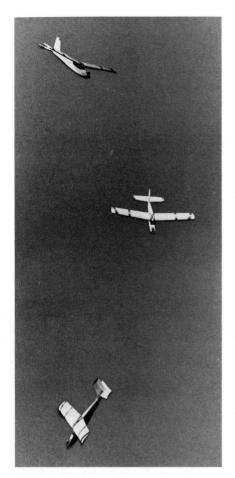

The spiral dive: Instinct tells you to apply up elevator, but doing so will only make the spiral tighter. The secret to a safe recovery is to roll the wings level and only then give up elevator.

Is this plane coming toward you or moving away? Unless it's close in and you can clearly make out the engine, spinner, and muffler, vision alone won't tell you which way the plane is moving.

In a spin, the plane rotates about its center of mass and drops.

to go down, which, by the way, is the technique you will use for landing approaches. Just don't overdo it or the plane will stall.

Stalls, spiral dives, and spins. Early in your RC career you will stall your plane. If you don't do so by accident, your instructor will talk you into it intentionally. Provided you have a reasonable amount of altitude to work with, stalls are no threat. Usually when a trainer stalls, it simply drops its nose and you just have to refrain from holding up elevator while it recovers airspeed. If you persist in holding up elevator, as you will want to, your plane will go into a spiral dive, or worse, a spin.

As soon as you realize the plane is stalled, let go of the elevator. The plane will dive a bit and build up airspeed. Once it has done that, add power, bring the nose back up to its normal attitude, and let the aircraft climb upstairs where it belongs before throttling back to cruise power.

Sometimes when a plane stalls, it drops off to one side. When this happens, you can recover the same way you would from any other stall, except before you pull the nose up, roll the wings level.

With practice you can tell when a plane is about to stall because the controls become mushy (that is, you have to feed in more control movement for a given response). In many planes, the ailerons stop working altogether before the wing stalls. When you see these symptoms, prevent a stall by dropping the nose with a little down elevator. This is difficult for the novice to do because every instinct tells you to pull back on the stick to gain altitude. Just remember that this particular instinct is wrong.

There is another way to prevent a stall — the one you will have to use on landing approaches, where most dangerous stalls occur, and where there is no room for a recovery dive. Like letting the nose drop, it is simplicity itself, and not nearly as unnerving. Just push the throttle control forward to increase power and make corrections to keep the nose from pitching up. As with all control movements, do this slowly and smoothly. If you suddenly add full power to a nearly stalled plane, the engine's torque may roll it over, or the engine, loaded up from idling, may quit.

Time and time again I've spoken of the spiral dive. It is easy to get into,

and fortunately, also easy to get out of if you know what you're doing. Here's how to recover:

1. Return the elevator to neutral.

2. Roll the wings level as the plane dives by pushing the right stick in the direction opposite the original turn. This will leave the plane in a straight dive.

3. Pull back on the elevator until the plane is flying straight and level, then ease up on the elevator to prevent the nose from rising too high.

As the nose rises to a stall, airspeed drops, lift is lost, and the plane begins to sink. If you also happen to be holding full up elevator and full aileron and rudder (both in the same direction) the plane may begin to rotate rapidly about its center of gravity with its nose down and tail up.

With some planes a spin is an inherently dangerous maneuver because it's difficult or impossible to get out of. Not so with a trainer. In fact, there's literally nothing to it. Just let go of both sticks for an instant and the plane will stop spinning and begin to dive. Once the spin stops, roll the wings level and ease in enough up elevator to bring the nose up to flying attitude, and you will have recovered.

An experienced RC'er preflights his plane, an important ritual that must be performed with the help of a checklist before each flying session.

8. Flight instruction

By the time your plane is ready to fly, you may or may not have rounded up a flight instructor whose radio equipment is suitable for use with a buddy cord and compatible with your system. If you can fly on a buddy system, do so.

If you're flying without a buddy system and get into trouble, the plane won't just float around upstairs; it will start down. If, as is likely, you forget to close the throttle at the first sniff of trouble, it may lose altitude at 100 feet a second or more, which leaves you little time to set things right. If the trouble starts at 200 feet, you could run out of time in two seconds, and almost certainly the plane will be down within five seconds if you haven't solved the problem. If you don't have a buddy box, you, your instructor, and your servos have only instants to save the plane.

It will likely be a race in two stages. First, you will do what you can, and second, if you fail, the instructor will take over, hopefully in time to avoid a crash. For your part, you must:
● Analyze the aircraft's flight to determine the problem.
● Decide how to correct the problem.
● Make corrections on the transmitter sticks.
● Wait for the servos to respond.
● Wait for the plane to respond to the control changes.
● Observe any change in the plane's flight.

● Decide whether to hand the transmitter to the instructor.
● If necessary, hand over the transmitter.

If you do hand over the transmitter, the instructor must then:
● Move the control sticks correctly (he will have decided what to do before you hand him the transmitter).
● Wait for the servos to move the controls.
● Wait for the plane to respond.

All that activity in two to five seconds doesn't leave time to negotiate whether to hand over the box, so before you get into this situation, agree with your instructor on the details of transferring control. Decide exactly what he will say, what you will say, where he will be standing, and how he wants the box presented to him.

Drill yourself ahead of time so that when the instructor calls for the transmitter, you hand it to him instantly and without question. Don't argue or wrestle or try to bargain, even if you think you can handle the situation yourself. You could be right, but so what? The most you can gain is a few seconds of flying time. If you're wrong — and students usually are — you're going to lose a plane and possibly hurt someone with it.

If the instructor doesn't yell for the box and you know you have a problem don't hesitate. Say "Take it!" and hold it out to him.

If you have a buddy system, there will be no danger of not handing over in time. You don't have to do anything. If the plane crashes because of pilot error, it will be your instructor's doing, not yours, and he's far less likely to make that mistake than you are.

Once you have the protocol established, it's time for preflight checks. A good instructor will go through them with you and he'll pull the wing off the plane and look inside to see that the glue joints are good and the radio and servos are properly installed. He has the experience, so don't resent this snooping, encourage it.

Draw attention to areas where you may have doubts yourself. I once preflighted a student's plane and found it in good shape until he pointed out that the elevator pushrod was not anchored by either a Z-bend or a pushrod connector. I don't know why, after doing everything else so well, he had made the mistake, but it was so unexpected I probably wouldn't have found it if it hadn't begun to worry him. Even if it had worried him to death and his pride had held sway, I wouldn't have known until after the crash what was wrong and he would have had the chance to build a new plane immediately. As it was, we fixed the problem and the plane flew fine.

Checking the plane. When I got into RC the preflight procedures at our field were relaxed — or to put it less kindly, inadequate. Now, thanks to former club president Larry Parfitt, we have stringent requirements for preflighting beginners' planes. Larry put together the checklist shown here for the club. It was distributed to members and is printed here with his permission.

To Larry's list I would add two points. First, before taking off, hold the plane vertical for ten seconds with the throttle wide open. If the engine slows down in this attitude, it is set too lean and you should open the needle valve until the engine will hold rpm in the vertical position. If it quits abruptly when you hold the nose up, chances are the clunk has become hung up; shake the plane violently to free the clunk. If that doesn't work, you will have to remove the tank.

My second point has to do with the battery. If possible, use an expanded-scale voltmeter (ESV) to measure the voltage of the onboard battery pack before takeoff. In a freshly charged 4-cell pack, this should be about 5 volts (1.25 volts per cell). If you don't have an ESV, at least make sure the batteries were charged the night before — not the previous week — and that they were charged for at least the time recommended by the manufacturer.

This maiden preflight will take a while and may uncover a problem or two that can't be fixed at the field. If it does, don't try to talk your instructor

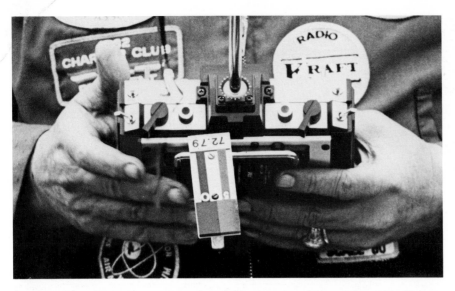

This pilot is range checking his radio system with the antenna collapsed before attempting to fly. Note the frequency pin clipped to the transmitter; club rules prohibit turning on the transmitter without this pin.

LARRY PARFITT'S MAIDEN FLIGHT CHECKLIST

INTERNAL
(Remove wing if attached.)

☐ 1. Check all servo mounts, servos, and servo arms for security.
☐ 2. Check that pushrods are secure.
☐ 3. Check that the receiver and battery are padded and secure.
☐ 4. Check for loose items that could foul servo or pushrod movement.
☐ 5. Check for fuel leaks. Is the tank area fuel-proofed?

WING

☐ 1. Check for breaks, warps, and other defects.
☐ 2. Ensure center section is adequately reinforced.
☐ 3. Check aileron pushrods and clevises (if used) before securing wing to aircraft.
☐ 4. Brief new pilots on adequacy of rubber bands.
☐ 5. After wing is in place, check for proper incidence and alignment as best you can.

ENGINE AREA

☐ 1. Is the fire wall area fuel-proofed?
☐ 2. Check engine mount, engine, muffler, and prop nut and spinner (if used) for security.
☐ 3. Check prop for nicks, cracks, or other defects. Brief new pilots on the importance of this check.
☐ 4. Check nose steering mechanism for security (if present).
☐ 5. Check engine for obvious thrust misalignment.

TAIL SECTION

☐ 1. Check vertical stabilizer, rudder, and clevis for security.
☐ 2. Check tail wheel for security (if present).
☐ 3. Check horizontal stabilizer, elevator, and clevis for security.

BALANCE

☐ 1. Balance airplane with fuel tank empty.
☐ 2. Show new pilots proper balance point and balance technique.
☐ 3. Explain danger of a tail-heavy aircraft.
☐ 4. Correct a tail-heavy plane before flight.

RANGE CHECK, ENGINE STARTING

☐ 1. Ensure that radio batteries have been properly charged.
☐ 2. When frequency pin is available, attach pin to antenna and range check the plane with antenna collapsed. Explain the importance of this check to new pilots.
☐ 3. Check to ensure that all flight controls and the throttle move smoothly and in the proper directions.
☐ 4. Check flight control surfaces for proper trim.
☐ 5. In an area far from the pits, fill the fuel tank, and start and tune the engine. Be certain new pilots understand how to adjust the engine.
☐ 6. Before flight, be certain to have a clear understanding with new pilots on how you want to handle transfer of the transmitter in case of trouble.

into flying, and don't let him talk you into taking that chance. Cart the plane home and keep it there until everything is right.

When it's finally ready, bring the plane to the field for another inspection and prepare yourself to enjoy the first flight from a distance. You may not even touch the controls this time, but you will at least find out for sure whether you built a flying machine or just something that looks like one.

Your plane's first flight. When the instructor is satisfied with the condition of your plane, make sure you've complied with the club's frequency rules, then turn on the radio system, crank up the engine, and hand the transmitter over to him (antenna fully extended). He will taxi to the end of the runway, point the model into the wind, and open the throttle. Your bird has arrived at the moment of truth. You'll see it gather speed and listen to the engine scream, and in a few seconds, if all goes according to plan, the wheels will break ground and the plane will begin climbing.

You will feel helpless and nervous. Even your instructor may be a tad nervous because maiden flights are a little unpredictable. As often as not, a new plane will lurch to the right or left on takeoff, or point its nose up into a stall attitude. Ninety-nine times out of a hundred, a good instructor will handle the problem without trouble, but there's always that hundredth time to worry about, when he's a split second too slow, the engine conks out on takeoff, or something else goes wrong.

You and the instructor will both be relieved (assuming all goes well) when the plane has climbed out and completed its first turn. At this point your instructor will climb another hundred feet or so and begin trimming. Since rudder and throttle have been set on the ground, he will only have to trim the ailerons and elevator in flight.

After trimming, the instructor should put the plane through a couple of left and right turns. He should also confirm that it generally handles well, recovers neatly from a stall, and the engine throttles smoothly. Then he can turn the controls over to you.

If the plane can't be properly trimmed in the air, the controls are too responsive, or some other problem arises, he'll have to land and make adjustments on the ground. No sense for you to fly before the plane is docile. You'll have a handful anyway.

When you take over the controls. When you finally take hold of the sticks, things will happen quickly. If you were learning to fly a full-size airplane, you would have a little time to get used to maintaining level flight before making serious changes in the plane's behavior. You could rock the wings a bit and get a feel for the eleva-

Before takeoff, hold the plane vertical with the throttle wide open to be sure the engine is not set too lean.

Instructor and student prepare to fly. The instructor (holding the transmitter) will next check out the plane's ground handling with a series of low- and high-speed taxi tests.

tor, rudder, ailerons, and throttle. But this is RC, and even a throttled-down trainer can fly out of sight in a few seconds. Almost as soon as you touch the sticks you're going to have to turn.

When you become an accomplished pilot you will sometimes use all four controls to turn the plane, but for now you can ignore rudder and your instructor will set throttle high enough that you won't have to touch it. You will use only the right stick for a while — you'll find this requires your full attention.

In describing how to turn, I will sometimes say to do one thing or another with the ailerons. If you have a four-channel airplane, this will be literally true. If you're flying a three-channel plane, use rudder wherever I say to use ailerons and you'll do fine.

When the instructor tells you to turn the plane, here's what to do:

1. Use the ailerons to roll the plane into a bank of 30 to 45 degrees. Remember that as long as you apply aileron pressure, the plane will continue to roll. It's not unusual for a beginner to roll the plane inverted because he forgets to neutralize the aileron stick

when the plane reaches the intended bank angle.

2. While you're establishing the bank, apply up elevator to steer the plane over the ground track you want. Go easy on both ailerons and elevator.

3. As the turn progresses, the plane may start to climb or dive. If it climbs, make the bank steeper. In the more likely event that it dives, roll in the opposite direction of the turn until it stops diving and maintains altitude. Turning requires constant adjustment of the bank angle — steeper to prevent climbing, shallower to prevent diving.

A new Eaglet taxis and takes off, climbing out gracefully.

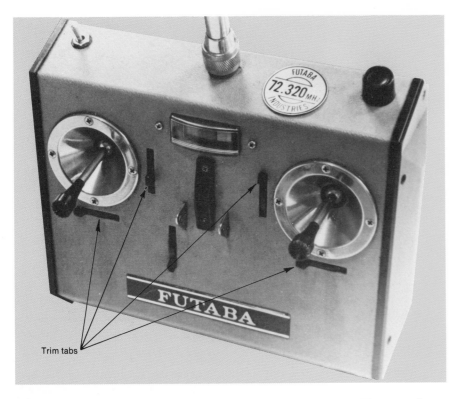

Trim tabs

After a maiden flight the trim tabs may be far off center, as here. The control surfaces should be adjusted and the tabs re-centered before the next flight. The idea is to set the control surfaces so that the plane flies straight and level with the trim tabs in their neutral positions. This often takes several flights.

An instructor (right) flies the plane while his student watches the transmitter sticks. Beginners are often surprised at how little the sticks move during most maneuvers.

You can't just leave the aileron stick in one position and forget it.

4. To end the turn, roll the wings level and simultaneously release the up elevator. Beginners have a tendency to forget to release the elevator, which causes their planes to zoom upward as the wings are leveled.

At first most of your turns will be 180 degrees — at least that will be your intention. You'll start with the plane going away from you and end with it coming more or less back toward you. Going out, things will feel natural, but coming back, with the plane pointed toward you, the controls will seem reversed, as if you're trying to fly in a mirror. It takes a while, but you'll get used to it. Until you do, though, remember that when the plane flies toward you, level the wings by moving the right stick to the side of the low wing.

For the first few flights, your major objective will be simply to keep from crashing, and you will frequently turn control back to your instructor. If you keep at it, though, you'll become proficient enough to begin putting the plane where you want it.

Flying an oval pattern. Once you've mastered the basics of turning and maintaining level flight, you can put them together to fly a nice oval racetrack pattern so the plane never gets too far away.

The oval pattern is easy enough if you can fly 180-degree turns. With the plane at about 300 feet and flying parallel to the runway 300 feet to your left or right, roll into a 30- to 45-degree bank, apply up elevator to set the radius of the turn, and adjust the bank to maintain altitude. Just hold the turn until the plane is headed the other way and is again parallel to the runway, headed back toward you. Fly the first straightaway until the plane is about 300 feet downrange in the other direction, perform another 180-degree turn, then fly the second straightaway to complete the circuit.

That's a brief description, but let me add some pointers on flying the straightaways. During these legs of the oval, especially during the one that is farthest from you, you may see only a silhouette of the fuselage and a small portion of the wing. If you see too much of the wing, the plane is banked and you will have to level it.

If you can see only the silhouette, or if the top and bottom of the wing are the same color, it's impossible to tell which wing is high and which is low unless you make control movements. Start by gently moving the aileron stick in the direction you think it should go, but be prepared to go the other way if you see much more of the wing after that control input.

The procedure isn't difficult, but there is one danger. If you move the aileron control too quickly or hold it too long, the plane may roll on its back, in which case you not only won't know which wing is higher, you'll also have to deal with reversed elevator control. If this happens, hand the box to your instructor instantly. You don't need a lesson in inverted flying at this point.

In 10 or 20 flights, you will practice the oval pattern dozens of times, turning both left and right (be sure to practice both ways). You will acquire the reflexes to fly the plane more or less where you want it to go, and will begin to wonder how it could have seemed so difficult in the first place.

Simple maneuvers. Obviously you're ready for greater things, so try a figure eight. Fly a 270-degree turn, and as you complete it, bank in the opposite direction and do a 360-degree turn. Finally, reverse the bank again and fly another 90 degrees before returning to level flight at the starting point. The figure eight is the easiest of maneuvers, yet for the beginner, it is difficult because it requires precise control to look good, and the only way to achieve that is practice.

Before you become good enough to land or even take off, you'll spend hours learning precise control of the plane. This can be boring, so like most novices, you'll probably want to try simple aerobatic maneuvers to liven things up. The inside loop is a good one to start with. It looks spectacular and there's nothing to it — well, not much.

Starting a couple of hundred feet up, apply full power, and when the plane gains a good head of steam, gradually apply up elevator. The plane will climb to a vertical attitude, continue over onto its back into an inverted dive, and finally an upright dive before returning to level flight.

As it goes inverted at the top of the loop, reduce the throttle to idle. There's no sense testing the wings' strength as you pull out. As the plane returns to level flight, open the throttle again, re-lease the up elevator, and fly away. Making loops is easy. Making pretty round ones is more difficult, and making several identical loops in the same spot is so difficult that most accomplished competitors avoid it. For present purposes, settle for a single loop that is fairly round. The roundness depends on the interplay of throttle and elevator. You'll have to learn this by trial and error, but you'll get the hang of it eventually.

There are other problems with loops that bedevil experts and beginners alike. If the plane is underpowered or if the flying surfaces are warped or out of line, the plane will tend to roll as you loop it, and the loop will look sloppy. In extreme cases, the plane will roll upright before completing the loop. There is no substitute for a well-built plane and adequate power, but there are ways to minimize the problems.

First, if the plane is underpowered, dive it steeply to gain speed before pulling up elevator. Using this technique, it is possible to loop some planes even after the engine shuts down, provided you start high enough. If the problem is a warp or a misaligned flying surface, you can compensate by using ailerons to level the wings as the plane flies through the loop. This takes practice and is never fully satisfactory, but it's better than no correction.

The other major cause of sloppy loops is pilot error. If the wings aren't level when you enter the loop, the result will not be pretty. You'll be pleasantly surprised at how your loops improve if you concentrate on leveling the wings before entry.

Another maneuver you will want to try is the Immelmann. This starts out like a loop, but when you get the plane inverted, you release the up elevator and use ailerons to do a half-roll. This will return the plane to the upright position and leave it headed in the direction opposite the one from which it began the maneuver. On most trainers

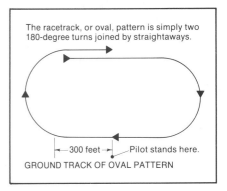

The modified Box Fly (Chapter 4) maintains altitude during a 180-degree turn. You will want to keep your plane much higher in the beginning.

The racetrack, or oval, pattern is simply two 180-degree turns joined by straightaways.

|← 300 feet →| Pilot stands here.

GROUND TRACK OF OVAL PATTERN

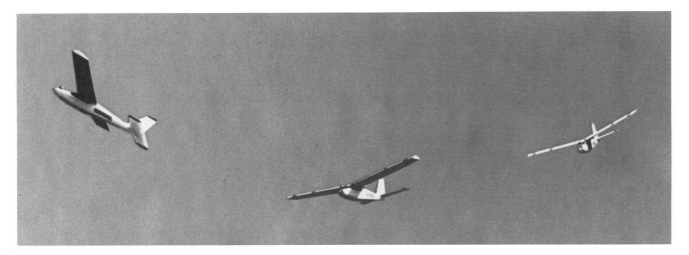

A plane turning as it comes toward you looks something like this. This one has begun to climb. To maintain level flight, the pilot should bank more steeply or use less up elevator. It's best to maintain a moderate flight speed while practicing.

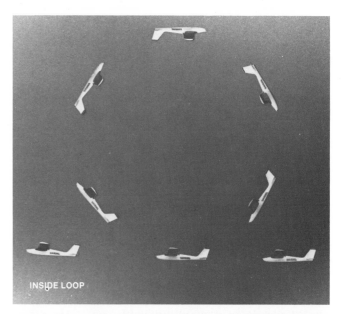
INSIDE LOOP

The modified Box Fly rolls into a turn at an altitude of about 8 feet. It is climbing, but left aileron will increase the bank and bring the nose even with the horizon in a second or so.

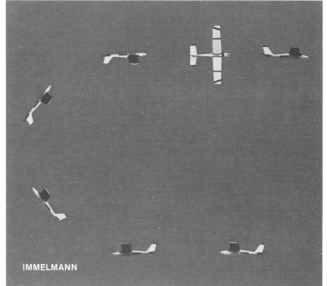
IMMELMANN

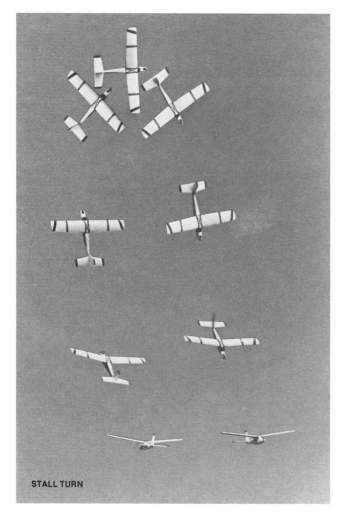
STALL TURN

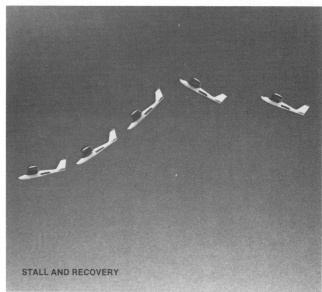
STALL AND RECOVERY

Practicing the stall turn, stall and recovery, inside loop, and Immelmann will help you gain confidence in the plane and your abilities. Many short practice periods are less fatiguing and more fun than marathon exercises. Also, fly so that the plane never passes in front of the sun.

52

New RC pilots sometimes try to stretch the glide by using up elevator — it doesn't work. Instead, the plane stalls and crashes short of the runway. If these pilots would add power instead of elevator, their planes would follow a course like that shown and would land safely.

On landing approaches you will see a succession of images that look something like these.

you can also do the half-roll using rudder, but if you have four channels, use ailerons only for a cleaner roll.

A common problem with this maneuver, especially on underpowered planes, is that it is difficult to maintain enough speed through the half-loop to perform the half-roll cleanly. The plane ends up inverted, but either stalled or so close to stalled that the ailerons are ineffective and will not roll it upright. This can be disconcerting to the novice, but fortunately the proper response is also the natural one. Simply pull lots of up elevator and complete the loop. As you do this, reduce power to idle.

If your plane has this trouble with the Immelmann, try things a little differently. First, make sure you have plenty of altitude and the throttle is wide open. Second, dive the plane steeply to gain speed before pulling up into the half-loop. Third, use elevator sparingly when executing the half-loop so you don't slow the plane more than necessary. If you use too little up elevator, the half-loop will be too big and you will lose speed because you have to climb too high in performing it. The ideal lies somewhere between the biggest and the smallest half-loop you can make, and you'll have to find it by trial and error. The best solution to the problem, however, is to install a bigger engine.

Another common problem with the Immelmann is that at the top of the half-loop the plane turns sharply to either the left or right as you begin to roll it upright. If you have this trouble, you're forgetting to neutralize the elevator before beginning the roll. If you can remember that, and if your plane is adequately powered, you'll quickly learn to fly clean Immelmanns.

A third simple aerobatic maneuver you'll want to try is the stall turn. Start in level flight at about 100 feet with full power. Use up elevator to pull the plane into a vertical climb, neutralize the elevator to maintain that attitude,

then chop the throttle. Wait until the plane is nearly stopped, give full rudder in the direction that will turn the plane away from you, and use a blast of throttle to blow air past the rudder.

If you time everything right, the plane should pivot about its center of gravity and end up pointed straight down. When it does this, release the rudder and allow the plane to dive until it regains flying speed. Try to follow the same trajectory you used in the vertical climb, and as you pull out at the same altitude where you started, open the throttle.

The toughest part of the stall turn is the pivot at the top. Mostly it's a matter of timing, which you will develop with practice, but there are a couple of other factors involved. For one thing, nose-heavy planes do the pivot easier. Unfortunately, that's about the only advantage of nose-heaviness. More important, when done in a crosswind, the pivot looks better if you do it into the wind. However, if this will turn your plane toward spectators or other pilots, it's not worth it.

Stalls. You can use these mild aerobatic maneuvers to break the tedium of learning the hard parts of flying, but most of your time will be spent on the pedestrian task of perfecting techniques for takeoff and landing. One job is to make friends with the stall.

There are several ways to stall an airplane, but the one you need to know about now is the one that occurs on takeoffs and landings. To check it out, climb to at least 200 feet, close the throttle almost to idle, and as the plane slows down, gradually apply enough up elevator to keep the nose high. Eventually, the plane will either just drop its nose or it will drop both the nose and one wing. Either way, it's going to lose altitude, and the secret of recovery is not to fight it. Release the up elevator to let the plane recover flying speed. Then roll the wings level, if necessary, and open the throttle to cruise setting.

When the plane regains flying speed, not before, use the elevator to raise the nose to level flight.

You'll master this recovery procedure quickly, but recovery is only part of the reason you need to practice stalls. For landings you'll have to develop a feel for when your plane is about to stall so you can prevent it from doing so.

Once you can recover easily, try to see how slow you can fly without stalling. Play around with elevator and throttle and try to maintain altitude at the slowest possible airspeed. At first you'll just want to make high altitude passes over the field, but after a while you can start playing with the ailerons. Try a 90-degree turn, for instance. You will notice first that your ailerons are not nearly as effective as they were at cruising speed and second, that once you get started into a turn, it's easy to slip into a spiral dive. If this happens, correct as you would for a stall that dropped off to one side. Neutralize the elevator, roll the wings level, add power, and when you get flying speed, pull the nose up.

When you have a feel for near-stall flying, try the oval pattern that way, then figure eights. You will quickly develop a sense of when the plane is about to go out of control and will find that you can bring it back from the edge by adding a little power.

It's important to know how to use power in low-speed turns because there will be times on landing approaches when you'll need to turn near the ground and can't afford a stall. To make the accompanying photo of the Box Fly in a low turn, I handed the camera to fellow RC'er Bill Cann, then took the plane up and circled back for a low-level pass over a predesignated spot on the field. As the plane neared the photo point, I gradually opened the throttle, simultaneously banking and applying up elevator. When the picture was taken, the throttle was nearly

You don't want your trainer's nose this high on takeoff. Do whatever is necessary to get it down nearer to the horizon.

wide open and I was holding almost full up elevator, but the bank was not yet steep enough. A little more left aileron put the nose down level with the horizon a second later, but of course, we didn't get that picture on film. Had I attempted this turn without increasing power, the plane would have dropped a wing into the ground and cartwheeled and I'd have been out a plane.

It will be a while before you try such a radical maneuver below ten feet, but since you will have occasion to make low-speed turns on landing approaches, you should know how to use the throttle as well as the ailerons and elevator. How much power and when to add it depend on the plane you're flying. You'll have to learn by trial and error at high altitude. Once you've mastered the technique, you'll definitely use it — not just for landings, but also to tighten up and smooth out those figure eights and other turning maneuvers.

There is one other secret to steep, slow turns. If you get too slow, the ailerons may become ineffective. You can cure this by adding power, but it will take a second or two before the plane responds. In the meantime you can control the bank angle with rudder. Most RC pilots never learn to do that, but it's worth the effort because it can save your plane.

Practicing landing approaches. Work on all these techniques until you become proficient at them and then begin working on landing approaches. At first you will just want to set up a glide, with no intention of getting anywhere near the ground. Start with the old oval traffic pattern, but as soon as you turn into the wind and aim at the runway, cut the throttle almost to idle and let the nose drop a bit to maintain flying speed.

Left to its own devices, the nose will probably drop too low, so use a little up elevator to bring it back up to an angle that gives a good glide, being careful

not to get too slow. In a perfect glide, airspeed is much lower than at cruise, but far enough above stall speed that the controls, especially the ailerons, are not mushy, and plane sinks at a rate that will bring it to earth just beyond the runway's end. If the controls become unresponsive, lower the nose or add a little power, whichever will keep you on the right glide path.

You will not get very low on your first few glides before the instructor tells you to add power and go around, but soon you will be descending below 100 feet and if your instructor is anything like me, he will yell a bit. The reason for this is that students concentrate so hard on the airplane that they don't even hear polite requests. Since there's not much time to get your attention if anything goes wrong at low altitude, most instructors yell, at least a little.

The five commands you are most likely to hear hollered are "Get the nose down!" — "Level the wings!" — "Cut the throttle!" — "Left!" — "Right!"

Keep those in mind as your instructor begins to talk you closer and closer to the ground and requires you to fly with greater precision. Responding without hesitation may be the difference between a near-miss and a month of rebuilding the plane.

Now back to the simulated landing approach. Assuming you've established a good glide, the plane should be coming toward you and sinking. By this time you will be holding a bit of up elevator, so if you want to stretch the glide, add a little power and the rate of sink will decrease. You can't do that by simply adding up elevator.

This is just gliding practice, not a real landing approach, so level off somewhere around 100 feet. To do that, increase power until the plane maintains altitude. Fly the length of the runway that way, then increase power, make your turn, and climb back to alti-

tude in preparation for another gliding approach. Practice until setting up a glide becomes second nature, then start bringing the plane lower and lower.

As the plane descends along the proper glide path, it will present a certain feel on the controls and a certain appearance. You will have to develop the feel through trial and error, but for the visual part, watch your instructor's landing approaches and imagine yourself at the controls. Ask him to fly approaches for you so you know exactly how they should look. Then let him talk you through several, telling you when to chop throttle, when to open it a bit, and when to increase or decrease up elevator. Repeat this procedure at lower and lower altitudes until you're leveling out at 25 to 30 feet.

Takeoffs. You should be getting pretty good by now. You're not ready to land yet, but takeoffs are easier, and it's time you started doing them. Pick a day when the wind is either calm or blowing straight up and down the runway. You don't need a crosswind for the first takeoff because steering can be difficult enough without complications.

The takeoff can be conveniently divided into four parts: takeoff roll, lift off, initial climb, and first turn.

During the takeoff roll your two main tasks are to advance the throttle smoothly and to steer the plane. Advancing the throttle is easy enough. Open it up as fast as it will go without the engine sputtering. You probably practiced this when you were learning to taxi. Hopefully, though, you didn't let the plane get anywhere near flying speed back then, so on your first takeoff roll you're trying something new.

The sensitivity with which your plane responds to the left stick will vary as the roll proceeds. At the beginning, when the speed is low, the nosewheel will steer just as neatly as it did when you practiced taxiing, but as you pick up speed, it will lose much of its traction and become less effective. On the other hand, the rudder will barely affect your course in the beginning, but will become progressively more important as speed increases.

You will have to contend with the fact that the plane's response to what you do on the left stick will vary and you will have to keep adjusting or lose control.

An experienced pilot can reflexively handle all sorts of steering problems because he will pay no attention to how far he has to move the stick and will focus all of his attention on where the plane is going. You'll get that way after a few dozen takeoffs, but for now you don't need surprises. Refer to the section in Chapter 3 that explains how to properly set up the steering; make sure yours is right before you take off.

It's a good idea to do some fast runs before committing yourself to a takeoff. Try two or three and if all seems well, go for it. But if, when you've decided the run is for real, the plane gets off its heading, abort the takeoff. Chop the throttle, taxi back, and try again. If you force the issue, you could easily break your plane or hit someone.

Let's suppose, though, that you steer a true course down the runway the first time. After about 50 or 60 yards on grass (less on pavement) you should have reached flying speed. Try a little up elevator and see what happens. If the plane doesn't break ground within a second, chop the throttle immediately. Don't wait till you reach the fence at the end of the field! Chances are you won't have this problem, since your plane has already taken off many times, but just in case, be prepared to abort.

Assuming the plane breaks ground on schedule, it will probably stick its

nose up into what will quickly become a stall attitude if you don't correct it. When this happens, you will have to perform what first seems to be a terrible, unnatural act. Five or ten feet off the ground you will probably have to ease the right stick forward. Most likely, when the nose gets down to the proper angle you will still be holding a little up elevator, but if you get the nose too high to begin with, you may have to give a little down — just enough to reduce the angle of climb below the danger level. Do this gingerly, and don't hold down elevator after the plane reaches the proper attitude. This is no time for a screaming dive. Do whatever it takes on the stick to get the right attitude.

This is one of those situations in which I usually yell "Get the nose down." It's hard for the student to force himself to do that, but if he does anything else, he's going to stall the plane under full power and crash. Gently push the stick forward until the plane is barely climbing. This completes the lift off.

Give the plane a couple of seconds to build up speed, then climb out at a steeper angle, but not so steep that the controls feel mushy. At 100 feet or so you will have completed the initial climb. All that's left to do is make a shallow, climbing, 180-degree turn to about 200 feet. Roll the plane into about a 30-degree bank, apply enough up elevator to set the radius of the turn, and let the plane go up to about 200 feet. Then level off, reduce the throttle to its cruise setting, and feel proud of yourself. You've finally taken off. In a few more sessions, you will learn to land, and a few sessions after that, you will solo.

Landings. By now you should be rea-

sonably comfortable with the glide and what you think of as the low pass over the field. I know 25 to 30 feet seems low, but if you're ever going to set the plane down, you'll have to get lower than that. All you have to do to land is set up a good glide and don't pull out till the plane is just about to touch down, at which point you should flare it a bit.

Of course, it's not that easy at first. For one thing, beginners who have perfect control at 100 feet or even at 30 sometimes go to pieces at 15 feet. Don't let the plane psych you; it flies the same way at 10 feet as at 500 — and you can see it better at 10.

Your instructor will talk you through the early landings. First he will have you fly the traffic pattern, and as you turn onto final, he will tell you to chop throttle. Actually, it's a good idea to leave the throttle open one notch if your plane will sink fast enough that way, because then your engine is less likely to quit if you have to go around and abruptly give full throttle. Your instructor will be giving commands to turn a little left or right, to apply a bit more up elevator, or to get the nose down. In fact, he may be screaming at you to get the nose down. It's only natural to feel that the plane should have its nose up, but don't let this happen. A nose-up attitude won't make the plane climb, it will only cause a stall, followed by a crash.

The prettiest possible way to approach is to glide exactly to the point of landing without touching the throttle, but don't try for that. It's not going to happen at first. The odds are your first approach will be too high. If it is, just add power and go around for another try. Next time come in a little low. If you have to be off, it's better to be too low on approach than too high, provided you're clear of all obstacles. You can always blip in a bit of throttle to stretch the glide as far as necessary.

As you're stretching the glide, make sure you have enough altitude to clear that last fence or tree along the glide path. You're working at the limits of human depth perception, so when in doubt, stay higher than the last obstacle until you're sure you've cleared it. If the plane suddenly disappears behind the fence, it's unlikely to reappear in one piece.

You shouldn't plan on actually landing on your first few approaches. Most students have problems. They usually don't get anywhere near the center of the runway and they come in too fast, too high, or both. You have to get a feel for it, which comes only with practice. Your instructor can help by telling you if you're starting the glide too high (or, less likely, too low), whether you're leveling off too soon or too late on your final approach, or are trying to land too fast. He will also tell you, as your plane

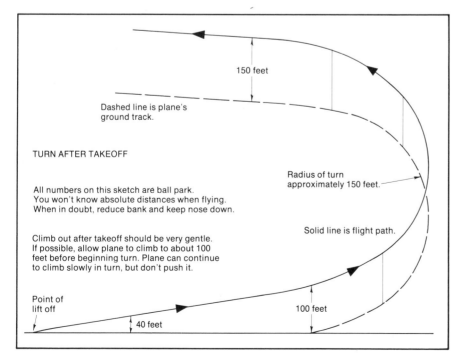

150 feet

Dashed line is plane's ground track.

TURN AFTER TAKEOFF

All numbers on this sketch are ball park. You won't know absolute distances when flying. When in doubt, reduce bank and keep nose down.

Radius of turn approximately 150 feet.

Solid line is flight path.

Climb out after takeoff should be very gentle. If possible, allow plane to climb to about 100 feet before beginning turn. Plane can continue to climb slowly in turn, but don't push it.

Point of lift off

40 feet

100 feet

passes over the near end of the runway, whether to add power and go around or just set it down.

When he finally tells you to touch down, let the plane glide till it's four or five feet up, then gradually flare by giving more up elevator. By the time the elevator takes effect, the plane will be only two or three feet above the runway.

The idea is to bring the nose up to the landing attitude; that is, the nosewheel slightly higher than the main wheels. Don't let the nose rise too high. It will try to do that as you flare the plane into level flight because it takes more up elevator to bring the nose up to this attitude than to keep it there at a given flying speed. As soon as it's into the flare position, you will probably have to back off a little on the up elevator. While you're doing all this, remember to keep the wings level. The instructor may be yelling about that, too.

As soon as you think you've gotten properly flared, the nose will begin to drop because the plane is slowing, and you will again have to increase up elevator. If you let the nose drop, you will get a rough landing. It's a delicate balance, but if you do it right, the plane will end up six inches or so off the deck and just a tad nose high and will skim the ground that way for 15 to 30 yards, bleeding off excess speed, before settling down to a smooth landing.

Nothing to it if you know what to do, but there is little chance your first landing will be graceful. Every now and then it happens. I even saw it happen once — pure luck. You've been flying mostly at 100 feet and higher, where a few feet one way or the other makes no difference. Just off the deck, though, the allowable errors are sometimes no more than two or three inches, and it will take time to get used to that.

You will make stupid mistakes on your early landings, but we all do. Just so you won't feel too bad, let me list a few of my own blunders. Most are typical beginner errors, but maybe by being forewarned you can avoid some of them.
• Leveled out at 5 feet (much too high). Stalled and crashed.
• Failed to level out in time. Crashed or at least landed hard.
• Decided my plane had cleared the fence at the east end of the runway and allowed it to descend below fence level. Surprise! It was still on the other side of the fence. Broke fuselage in half.
• Lined up a little crooked on approach, but decided to land anyway. Perfect touchdown. Plane ran into tree at side of runway.
• Landed plane in weeds at far side of runway. Minor damage.
• Destroyed plane in elm tree I thought was farther away than it was.
• Came in too hot, flared with too much up elevator. Plane climbed from ground

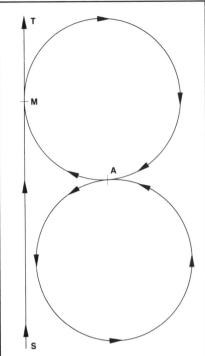

The plane flies from **S** to **M**, where it begins a right turn. This turn continues for 270 degrees to **A**; the plane then makes a 360-degree left turn which ends when the plane returns to **A**. At this point the plane does a 90-degree right turn to **M**, where it levels out and flies off in the direction of **T**.

FIGURE EIGHT (TOP VIEW)

level to six or eight feet, stalled, and crashed. Major repairs required.

You will make some of these mistakes, but there's no need to make all of them. You will have trouble at first knowing when to begin your flare, and at best that will cause rough landings. Practice is the only way to get the hang of it. You are going to come in too high or too hot or both. When you do, don't try to land; just go around and come in lower and slower next time. That engine you so painstakingly tuned will come in handy for this.

You will sometimes come in at an angle to the runway. If you do, don't land. As soon as you realize the problem, add power and straighten your plane out as it climbs back upstairs for another try. If it is headed toward people and you are not certain you can turn sharply enough to avoid them, immediately give full down elevator. Sure, that's the end of your plane. So what? You can get another plane. But if you kill somebody (and you can) it's going to take the edge off your enjoyment of the hobby.

Don't give in to the urge to save your plane in this situation. I know that's the natural instinct, but like many others, that instinct is wrong. To be on the safe side, go over this scenario in your mind every so often and imagine yourself deliberately crashing your plane. Then, if the time ever comes, you won't hesitate. You will probably never find yourself in this situation, but if you do,

program yourself to dump the airplane.

The peskiest problem you'll face in learning to land is deciding when your plane has cleared the last obstacle along its glide path and can be safely let down. I can set the plane down within a foot or two of the runway center line every time, but it's hard to be sure when I've cleared the last fence or tree and can let down safely. If that were just a result of poor depth perception on my part, I wouldn't bother you with it. But it's not just me. It's all of us. Human stereoscopic vision is great for close work, but isn't worth a hoot 50 yards away.

Several years ago, one of our club's hotshot pilots had a bomb drop apparatus on one of his planes. He used it to drop a long orange crepe paper streamer from about 400 feet. Thereupon, he and two other experts pounced on the ribbon — or rather, they tried to pounce on it. The ribbon slithered safely to the ground with planes buzzing all around it. This so frustrated our crew that they spent the rest of the afternoon chasing the fool ribbon and never touched it. Their eyes couldn't tell them within 50 feet how far out that ribbon was, and you will have the same problem trying to figure out exactly how far your airplane is from an obstacle along the glide path. Try to get as close to the obstacle as you can because the closer you are, the better your depth perception works.

(You've probably figured out that our experts could have cut that ribbon by flying a straight line from themselves to it. You're right, but that wouldn't have been sporting. Besides, those who tried missed.)

Solo. Eventually, all that I've written in this chapter will become second nature to you, but before that, you'll have some hair-raising flights. If you don't believe me, try a landing now. Scary, isn't it? Sooner or later you'll get the plane down without breaking anything (props don't count) and by then you'll have successfully done all the maneuvers you need to fly by yourself. Don't do it yet. Get at least a dozen tolerable landings under your belt before cutting the buddy cord. When you reach that point, tell your instructor you want to try a solo flight, and if he agrees, go to it.

The solo itself is nothing new, and you've got a big advantage over the student pilot in a full-size plane. Once he's taken off, he's really alone and either has to fly or die. You can still call for help if you need it. You shouldn't have any trouble, but if you do, don't hesitate to yell for an expert. You can solo the next time or the time after that, but only if you still have a plane.

Now for the solo itself. You've flown the same plane dozens of times before, but this time is different. Your instructor is strangely silent. You preflight

The takeoff should look like this. Notice that the nose is held low, allowing the plane to fly itself off the ground and gain airspeed before beginning a steeper climb.

The modified Box Fly sinks toward the runway on a landing approach. The right wing (your left) is a little low and should be brought level with left aileron.

(Left) This plane is flared just about perfectly on its final landing approach. (Above) This one is nose-high and may stall before getting close enough to the ground.

the plane, start the engine, and taxi to the runway's end as you have before. You stop briefly to wipe the sweat from your palms. You look left and right and up in the sky. All clear. You open the throttle all the way. The engine screams. You watch the plane bump over the grass, gaining speed. Automatically, you apply tiny rudder movements to keep it straight.

You ease back on the stick and the nose rises. You hesitate an instant, waiting for someone to yell "Get the nose down!" But no one yells, and finally you push the nose down on your own. Your mouth is full of cotton. Your hands could be steadier. So could your knees. You level the low wing, climb to 100 feet, do your 180-degree turn, then level the wing again, climb to 200 feet, level off, cut the throttle back to cruise setting, and take a deep breath.

The flight plan calls for a couple of oval patterns before beginning your landing approach. You will normally

fly much longer than this, but the first time you may have to make several approaches to the field before you get one just right. That could eat up all your fuel and force you to land from a poor approach, or even with a dead engine. So you do two left-handed patterns, noting that they are pretty ragged compared to what you're used to, and prepare to land.

You turn onto final and chop the throttle. Did you start too high? Too low? Are you lined up with the runway? You at least know the answers: too high and not even close to lined up. You open the throttle and fly another traffic pattern. Damn! Still too high. One more time. Now you're low enough, maybe too low, and lined up correctly. Stretch the glide with a little power if you have to.

The instructor says nothing, but you decide to go for it. This is it. Just goose that engine for a second to clear the fence and you'll make it. Don't glide too

fast, but definitely don't glide too slow. Stay lined up with the field. Get that low wing up — move the stick toward that side. Blip in a little more power. Twenty feet up now. Never realized how fast this thing was. Ten feet up. Cleared the fence for sure. Throttle all the way closed down. Eight feet up and the plane just passed by. Start the flare now. Easy on the elevator. Quick, level the wings again. More up elevator. Not that much! Plop! Not a graceful landing, but everything seems to be in one piece and you've soloed!

All the hours of building and making mistakes in the air have paid off — all that time when you wondered if you could ever handle the thing. Well, you've done it. In a few more sessions you'll be flying without an instructor, but don't rush it. That first landing was a little shaky. It won't hurt to have an old-timer keep an eye on you till you're sure you can get up and down regularly without breaking your airplane.

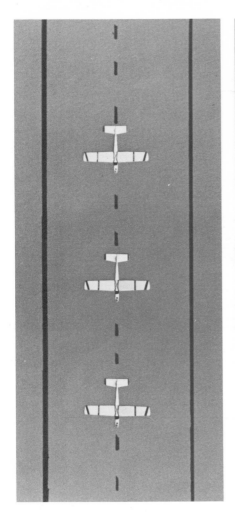
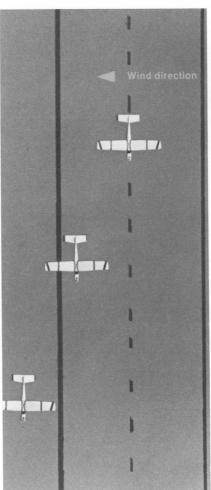
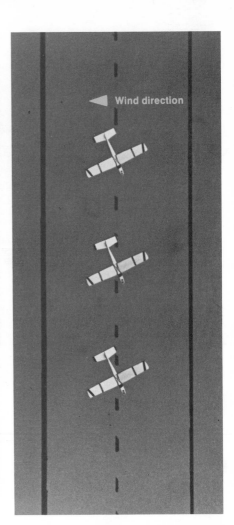

(Left) In perfectly calm air the plane follows its nose and flies straight ahead over the runway center line. (Center) However, in a crosswind the plane's ground track lies at an angle to the direction the nose points; the plane drifts to the left. (Right) So, to keep the plane over the runway center line in a crosswind, the pilot must crab into the wind.

9. Special flying techniques

You already know how to fly the airplane, but there are situations in which special techniques will come in handy. Specifically, there are ways to react when your engine quits in the air or when the wind howls, making conventional landing procedures all but useless, or when you've made a too-high approach and for one reason or another (a dead engine, for example) don't want to go around again. This chapter concentrates on techniques for handling high winds and dead engines; it will help you acquire the skills to better cope not only with these problems, but with normal flying as well.

Early in your RC career you fly only in the lightest of winds because it's safer. You gain some mastery over the plane and begin to feel confident. This eventually seduces you into flying on a breezy day, and suddenly you lose all the ability and confidence you so carefully built up. The plane won't fly with-

in 50 yards of where you aim it and it bounces around, climbing and diving and wallowing and speeding up and slowing down and flying crooked.

One problem is gusts that force frequent control adjustments. More disturbing, though, the plane just isn't going where it's aimed. That oval pattern you worked so hard to perfect is now unrecognizable. The plane drifts toward you or away from you even when you don't touch the controls. When you turn away from the wind, it dives. Downwind it goes like the hammers; into the wind, it barely crawls. Your mouth gets dry and you wonder how you're supposed to land.

Flying in strong winds is exciting, but you'll have a better chance of doing it safely if you understand how the wind alters the plane's ground track and how to correct for these alterations.

Imagine yourself in a rowboat on the Amazon River. You've rowed out of

sight of shore so you can test your new radio control boat in peace and quiet. You slip the little model over the side and steer it through all sorts of maneuvers. Nothing to it. Want to do a circle? Just give it some rudder and it does the circle for you. Pretty, isn't it?

Well, yes and no. From your point of view it's pretty, but how does it look to that diver braced against the current on the river bottom? He doesn't even see a circle. As he sees it, the boat is performing a lopsided spiral that's taking it downstream.

You see a circle because both you and your boat are drifting with the current. The diver doesn't see this because he's tied to the riverbed and doesn't follow the current. Being out of sight of land, you can't detect the current, but it threatens to bowl him over.

Suppose now that your transmitter is waterproof and that you drop it down to the diver, who then turns your model

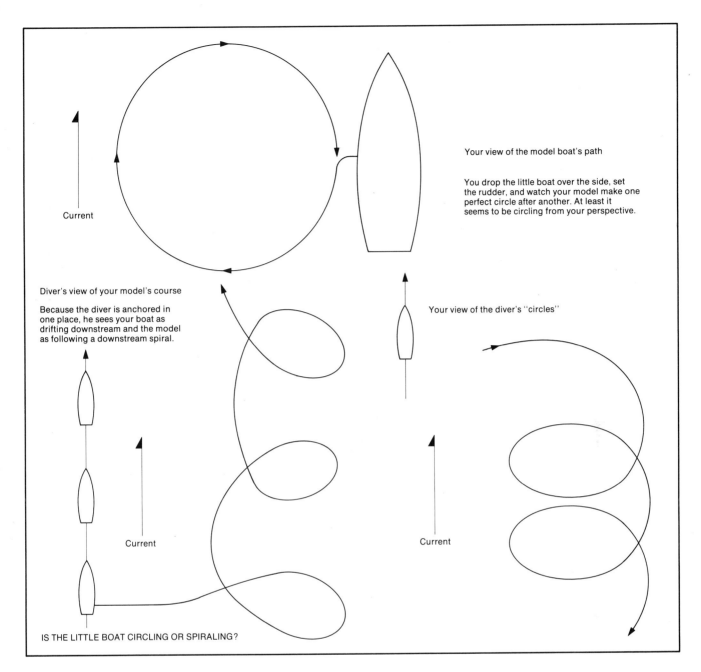

Current

Your view of the model boat's path

You drop the little boat over the side, set the rudder, and watch your model make one perfect circle after another. At least it seems to be circling from your perspective.

Diver's view of your model's course

Because the diver is anchored in one place, he sees your boat as drifting downstream and the model as following a downstream spiral.

Your view of the diver's ''circles''

Current

Current

IS THE LITTLE BOAT CIRCLING OR SPIRALING?

boat in what looks like a circle to him. He can't do this by simply holding the rudder in one position as you did at the surface. He will have to make adjustments constantly to hold what he sees as a circular course. That's not how it will look to you: You'll see a lopsided spiral headed upstream.

When you fly RC, you're the diver, not the man in the boat. If you want to fly a circle in a heavy wind, you'll have to make adjustments constantly. When you've flown in relatively calm weather, you've been able to act as if you were the man in the boat, just as the diver could have done had he been working from the bottom of a calm lake instead of a flowing river. If the air is calm, you don't have to keep playing with the controls. But when you're flying in a high wind, you have to fly all the time. You will always be evaluating the plane's ground track and making corrections. If you try to make circles us-

ing the control pressures that work in calm air, you'll get a lopsided spiral headed downwind.

To fly your circle in a strong wind, you'll need to make more adjustments than I can enumerate here, but all of them will be variations of a few kinds. I'll describe these in order from the simplest to the most complex.

Crabbing. Suppose that the air is calm and you make a pass over the runway, flying from east to west at 50 mph. Nothing to it. You just get the plane pointed the right way and leave it alone. Now suppose a wind comes up and blows from the south at 10 mph. If you fly as you did on the earlier pass, the plane will drift to the north at 10 mph.

Since you want to go straight up and down the runway, you'll have to point the nose into the wind a bit — 11.5 degrees in this case. This does not mean you have to fly the plane in a bank. You will bank to get the plane cocked

into the wind, but then you will level the wings because the plane will be crabbing, not turning. In fact, with respect to the air it will fly a straight line following its nose. But you're interested in its ground track, which will also be a straight line — but up and down the runway, not in the direction the nose points.

The biggest secret of flying in the wind is to ignore the direction the nose points and follow the ground track. Under the conditions specified above, your model will go exactly from east to west if, and only if, you crab the nose 11.5 degrees into the wind. For a stronger wind or a slower plane, the angle will be greater; for a slower wind or a faster plane, it will be less. Just crab as much as it takes to fly the line you want. Once you get the idea, it's not difficult.

Turning in a wind. Now let's look at some simple turns. Assume the wind blows from north to south and the

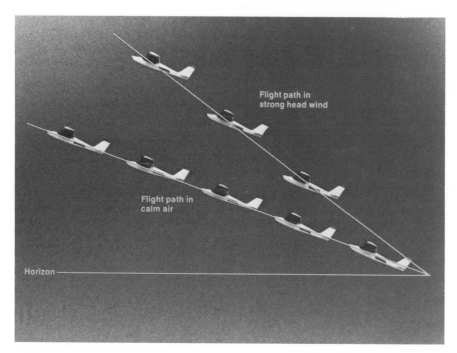

Flight path in
strong head wind

Flight path in
calm air

Horizon

At a given angle of attack, the plane will climb more steeply (as seen from the ground) in a head wind. With a tail wind, the perceived climb will be shallower.

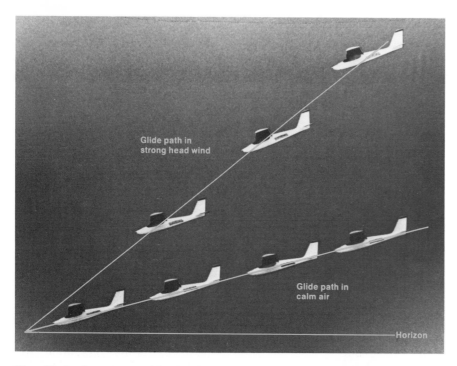

Glide path in
strong head wind

Glide path in
calm air

Horizon

The glide is also steeper with a head wind (and flatter with a tail wind).

plane starts out headed due north into it. Imagine how you will move the controls to make a 90-degree left turn. If you use the control movements that work in calm air, you will turn more sharply than you had intended.

With respect to the air, it will be a perfect turn, but you're not the man in the boat. You're the diver, remember? You see things differently because you don't move with the current. To make the curvature right for you, you have to decrease the amount of bank and up elevator as you progress through the turn. Stop the turn while the nose is

still sufficiently cocked into the wind.

If you try to make a 90-degree turn with a tail wind, you run into the same problem except that things are reversed. This time the wind will cause your normal turn to appear stretched out, so you'll have to turn tighter and you'll have to keep turning until the nose has passed through more than 90 degrees and is crabbed into the wind.

I could write page after page on the details of different maneuvers performed at different angles to the wind, but that wouldn't help you a bit. You have to understand what you're up

against, as illustrated by the crabbing and turning examples, and then practice flying by the ground track — not the direction the nose points.

Maintaining altitude in turns. So far I've ignored one problem that most new fliers have. Everybody knows that when a plane turns into the wind, especially if it has a flat-bottom airfoil, it automatically climbs, and that when it turns away from the wind, it loses altitude. What everybody does not realize is that neither the wind nor the flat-bottom airfoil is responsible for these altitude changes. The plane climbs when it turns into the wind because an inexperienced pilot reduces the bank upon seeing the plane turn too sharply and does not simultaneously reduce up elevator.

When the plane turns away from the wind, a novice tends to increase the bank to prevent the turn from being stretched out. The plane ends up banked too steeply for the power applied, and loses altitude. I don't know why beginners make these errors, but virtually all do.

After writing this section, I put it to the test with a student. He was flying a Goldberg Eagle, which is a nice, stable trainer with a flat-bottom airfoil, and he was blessed with an almost perfectly steady wind of 10 mph or so. Like other novices, he was having problems holding altitude during turns. Every time he pointed the plane into the wind, the thing climbed, and every time he turned downwind, it lost altitude. He'd never flown in wind before and he thought something was wrong with the plane.

Worried, he handed me the transmitter and was amazed to see the up and down gyrations stop immediately. I handed the transmitter back to him with instructions to set his plane into a gentle turn on the downwind side and to freeze on the controls. With a plane as stable as the Eagle, you can do this for a while. He watched as the plane completed the downwind part of the turn and then headed into the wind. It did not climb. Then he turned downwind and it did not dive.

It didn't make neat turns, either. The downwind turn was stretched out and the upwind turn was all bunched up. However, once my student understood the problem, he learned to pull his downwind turns tighter without losing altitude and to stretch his upwind turns without climbing. He had learned the secret of watching both the ground track and the altitude and in no time at all found that he could control both simultaneously.

When the plane started to sink on the downwind leg because he was turning tightly with respect to the air, he applied more power. When he reduced the bank to turn into the wind, he also reduced the pressure on his elevator control. He began to anticipate prob-

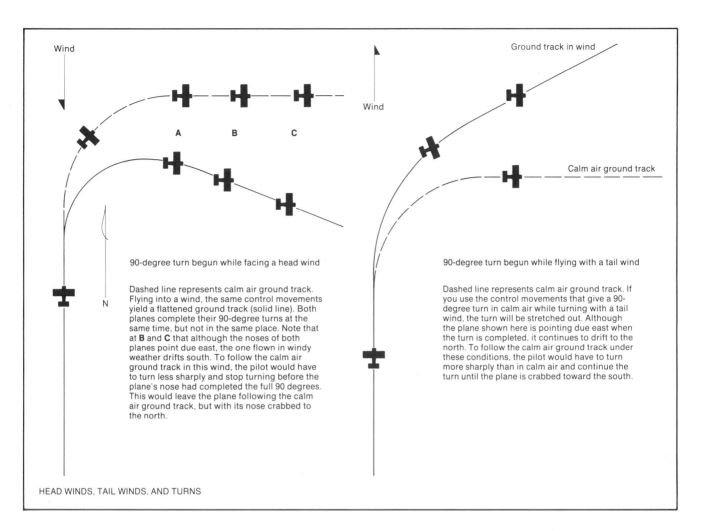

Wind

Wind

Ground track in wind

A   B   C

Calm air ground track

N

90-degree turn begun while facing a head wind

Dashed line represents calm air ground track. Flying into a wind, the same control movements yield a flattened ground track (solid line). Both planes complete their 90-degree turns at the same time, but not in the same place. Note that at **B** and **C** that although the noses of both planes point due east, the one flown in windy weather drifts south. To follow the calm air ground track in this wind, the pilot would have to turn less sharply and stop turning before the plane's nose had completed the full 90 degrees. This would leave the plane following the calm air ground track, but with its nose crabbed to the north.

90-degree turn begun while flying with a tail wind

Dashed line represents calm air ground track. If you use the control movements that give a 90-degree turn in calm air while turning with a tail wind, the turn will be stretched out. Although the plane shown here is pointing due east when the turn is completed, it continues to drift to the north. To follow the calm air ground track under these conditions, the pilot would have to turn more sharply than in calm air and continue the turn until the plane is crabbed toward the south.

HEAD WINDS, TAIL WINDS, AND TURNS

lems and to feed in corrections so those problems never became visible. He had learned two cardinal rules of RC flying:
• Anticipate changes in control requirements.
• Constantly monitor ground track and altitude changes and adjust control inputs as necessary.

Takeoffs and landings in a wind. It doesn't take long to master the high-altitude part of windy weather flying, but down low the story is different. The good news is that if the wind is steady, landings and takeoffs are easier than they are in calm air. The first piece of bad news is that strong winds are usually gusty, and while gusts normally cause takeoff problems only for underpowered airplanes, they turn landings into nightmares for everyone. The second piece of bad news is that sometimes strong winds are crosswinds, which make both takeoff and landing difficult.

Let's start with the good news, though, that strong, steady winds make landings and takeoffs safer. In a really strong wind, you'll have to carry your model to the runway's end because if you try to taxi, it will be blown over. But once you set it down with its nose pointed into the wind, it will stay there. Now open the throttle all the way and notice that the plane is almost instantly airborne. Even though you haven't let the nose rise too high, it's

climbing at an alarming rate with no indication of an impending stall. The plane is nowhere near stall because although its ground speed may be only 10 or 15 mph, its airspeed is already 30 to 35 mph.

On the rare occasions I get the chance to fly in a strong, steady wind, I have all sorts of fun with landings. For example, I don't worry about losing an engine on final approach because I keep the plane upwind all the time. If the engine conks out, the wind carries the plane back to me quickly and with a flat glide.

When it reaches the end of the runway, I can turn sharply back into the wind and land almost vertically. Some-

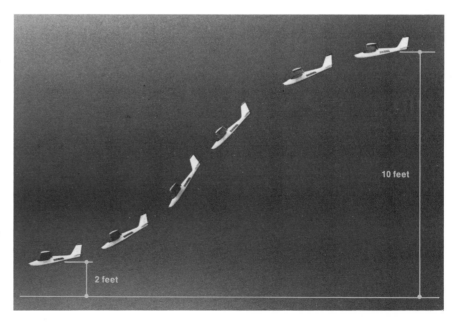

10 feet

2 feet

The dangers of turbulent air can be minimized by diving to just above the runway.

Two hundred feet up and no power, yet this plane can land safely if the pilot flies by the book.

This Eaglet has just made it. Had the pilot hesitated another tenth of a second in deciding on his approach, the plane would have crashed short of the runway.

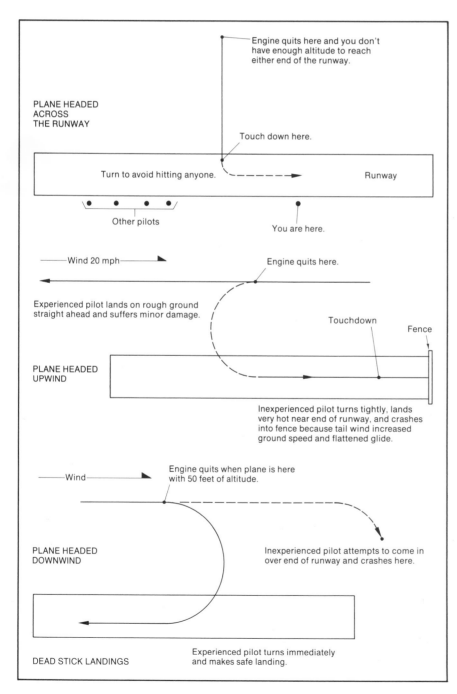

Engine quits here and you don't have enough altitude to reach either end of the runway.

PLANE HEADED ACROSS THE RUNWAY

Touch down here.

Turn to avoid hitting anyone.   Runway

Other pilots

You are here.

Wind 20 mph   Engine quits here.

Experienced pilot lands on rough ground straight ahead and suffers minor damage.

Touchdown

Fence

PLANE HEADED UPWIND

Inexperienced pilot turns tightly, lands very hot near end of runway, and crashes into fence because tail wind increased ground speed and flattened glide.

Wind   Engine quits when plane is here with 50 feet of altitude.

PLANE HEADED DOWNWIND

Inexperienced pilot attempts to come in over end of runway and crashes here.

DEAD STICK LANDINGS

Experienced pilot turns immediately and makes safe landing.

times, even when the engine runs fine, I kill it and set up my glide almost over the runway's end. All that's necessary is to make the glide steeper to compensate for the lack of engine power. Then, if the wind is strong enough, the plane can descend vertically for a landing with zero ground speed.

Even if you don't care about vertical landings, it's nice to be able to make your turn onto final close to the field and as high as you like, knowing that it's all but impossible to overshoot the field, and that even if you do, your plane will "crash" at no more than a few miles per hour.

When you make such landings, though, there is one caution to keep in mind. When you touch down, make sure the plane is ready for the last bit of up elevator before you flare it. Once again, the wind will try to fool you. In a 20 mph wind (or higher) your model will be all but stopped with respect to the ground before it reaches stall speed. Since you tend to judge when to flare by the plane's ground speed (you will eventually make this judgment on the basis of control feel) it's easy to believe it's time to flare before it is.

The result of this misperception is that you give a little up elevator and your plane, instead of flaring, abruptly climbs five or ten feet. Then it stalls and crashes. The surest way to prevent this is to touch down with virtually no flare. This works fine for planes with tricycle gear, but if you have a taildragger, you may have to flare a bit before the wheels touch to keep the plane from nosing over. If so, do it cautiously and back off if the plane starts to climb.

Flying in gusty weather. So far we've considered only steady winds. Unfortunately, they are rare. Most of the time, if the wind is up, your model will be bounced around by gusts, and takeoffs and landings will resemble Russian roulette. The first bit of safety equipment you should have for these

Both the Falcon (above) and Eagle (right) easily reached the runway without power and landed safely.

conditions is a powerful engine. Even an underpowered plane will get off quickly in a strong wind, but how fast it can climb is determined not by the wind, but by how much horsepower the propeller delivers.

An underpowered plane will spend more time down low where a gust can knock a wing into the ground, or just cause a stall when there's no altitude for recovery. High-powered planes are vulnerable only for a second or two because they quickly get far above stall speed and climb to a safe altitude.

I've made the gusty weather takeoff with an underpowered plane sound risky, and it is, but if you insist on flying such a plane in turbulent weather, a couple of precautions will improve the odds. First, don't lift off until the plane is way above minimum flying speed. This is insurance that when it finally breaks ground it will have enough airspeed for good aileron control and be far enough above stall that a sudden gust will not crash it. The extra speed is also stored energy that can be used to climb high enough that even a severe gust cannot cause the plane to drag a wing. Those precautions will help, but it will still seem like a long time before you get it to 100 feet and relative safety.

If yours is a high-powered plane, don't be too smug about flying in the wind. You have a big advantage on the takeoff, but when it comes to landings, your edge is much less. As you approach the ground, you pass through a window of vulnerability in which a strong gust can crash the plane no matter how good a pilot you are, and the best you can do is try to make that window as small as possible.

The first thing to do is come in hot. Leave the throttle slightly open, come in at a steeper angle, and touch down faster than usual. Often the air at ground level is much calmer than higher up, so it's a good idea to dive

through the last turbulence from 10 feet or so, pulling out just off the deck. This minimizes the time spent in the most dangerous turbulence, and because of your higher airspeed, allows better control while you're in it.

Flying in high winds can be fun, but there are no guarantees. A few years ago I developed a reputation as the club pilot most willing to fly in impossible weather. I also rebuilt a lot of smashed airplanes. There's no way to put hard numbers on when a wind is safe. Sometimes 25 mph is a lark and sometimes 15 mph will kill you. At our club field, a 15 mph wind from the south reduces landings to badly calculated risks because of the way the air swirls over nearby trees. On the other hand, I've flown there in a west wind so strong that it was possible (and fun) to do consecutive rolls in place.

Probably the best rule is to see how other pilots fare in any given wind, and if they do all right, try it yourself. But even if no one else goes up, eventually you're going to try it yourself. Flying RC is supposed to be exciting, isn't it? Well, a good gusty wind will ensure that it is.

Dead stick landings. Sooner or later your engine will quit while the plane is still in the air. Maybe you run out of fuel, maybe the needle valve isn't set quite right, but whatever the cause, you find yourself with a plane in the sky and no power. What to do?

Most of the time, there's no reason for panic. If the plane has enough altitude to reach the field and you fly reasonably well, you're going to get it down in one piece. But don't be complacent. The plane will touch down in a matter of seconds and in that time there's work to be done.

As soon as you realize the engine has stopped, yell "dead stick" at the top of your lungs. This warns other pilots and anyone who might be dawdling on the field that you're coming in and that it

is up to them to stay out of your way. Of course, you'll still have to make sure no one is on the runway, and if someone is, you'll have to land elsewhere, curse him though you may. But yelling "dead stick" should clear a path for you.

The second thing you do, even as you yell, is begin to turn the plane toward home and decide on the exact approach. It is critically important to head for the field immediately because every second of delay reduces your gliding range by 50 or 75 feet. It is also critically important to decide whether you can make a dead stick landing along the usual into-the-wind approach, whether you will have to come in from the other side for a downwind landing, whether the best you can do is barely make the middle of the field for a crosswind landing, or whether you'll miss the field entirely and have to settle for the flattest off-field spot you can reach.

If there is any doubt about whether you can make the most desirable approach, scrap the idea and go for second best. For example, if you can't be sure of reaching the end of the runway where you can make the usual approach into the wind, but know you can get to the other end, go with the sure bet and prepare yourself for a downwind landing. If both options are chancy, head for any spot on the field you can reach. If there is no way to get to the field, come in slowly, level the wings, and land wherever you can.

Each case is different, but there are patterns and rules of thumb to go by. The first rule is to head for home instantly. Even if you have enough altitude to land anywhere on the field, you should still get back immediately. Too many RC pilots, when they find they have extra altitude, do all sorts of turns far from the runway, only to discover the wind has shifted or they've miscalculated and the field is now out of reach.

There is also a tendency to set up a

To the RC pilot, one loop of an S-turn looks something like this. If need be, it can be stretched even farther to the left (the plane's right) to kill more altitude while covering the same distance toward the runway.

Three stages of entering a slip: (a) The plane is in level flight. (b) The pilot rolls the plane with the rudder. (c) Finally, right aileron raises the low wing while left rudder holds the fuselage into the airstream, increasing the drag and the rate of descent without increasing airspeed.

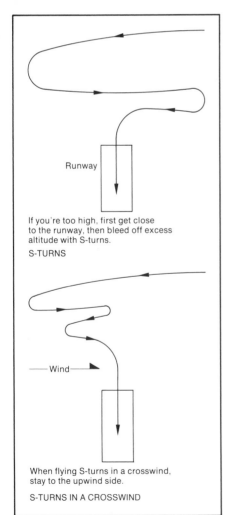

Runway

If you're too high, first get close to the runway, then bleed off excess altitude with S-turns.

S-TURNS

Wind

When flying S-turns in a crosswind, stay to the upwind side.

S-TURNS IN A CROSSWIND

long, leisurely final approach, as one might do if the engine were still running. Again, if you misjudge, or if the wind shifts, you can come up short of the field and there's no way to extend the glide. You're flying dead stick, and if you come up short, you're dead.

Since it's easier to misjudge distance when the plane is far away, get it in where you can see it better. Sure, it will be too high for a straight-on landing approach, but as long as you're above any obstacles, you can bleed off the excess altitude with an S-turn or two. If your final S-turn brings you over the runway's end a little high (if you have to be off on a dead stick, be sure you're high, rather than low) you can make final adjustments by slipping the plane. More about slipping later, but the easiest and most important tool for killing altitude is the S-turn, which is just what it sounds like. You will rarely have to make more than one or two "esses." In extreme cases you may have to fly 150 feet or so in one direction, then fly a 180-degree turn and go the other way for a while.

If you're flying S-turns in a crosswind, stay on the upwind side of the approach. If you need to get back to the field in a hurry, you'll get a boost from the wind if you're turning away from it, but if you're turning into it, it will slow you down and cost more altitude for the same distance.

Most RC pilots, if they're way too high, will circle somewhere along the

glide path to burn up extra altitude. This is a terrible idea because if you begin a circle and then realize you're getting too low, your plane may still be out there flying away from the field, losing altitude you need to conserve, and the only options you have are to reverse the circle or complete it. Stick with the S-turns. That way you're never flying directly away from the field and it won't take long to get going the right way if you have to change plans.

The slip. If you come in a little high after finishing the last S-turn, and if you're flying a high-wing trainer, you can slip the plane to get rid of that last bit of extra altitude. Caution: If you're flying a low-wing aerobatic plane, forget about the slip. The slip depends on the ability of the rudder to roll the airplane and aerobatic planes are designed so they don't roll with rudder.

The slip is an easy technique to learn and is useful for fine tuning your glide path just before landing, whether your engine is running or not, but it's especially handy for dead stick landings. The idea is to move the control surfaces so that the plane flies cocked to the glide path. This puts more of the fuselage into the airstream and greatly increases drag, which allows you to increase the rate of descent without increasing speed.

You perform the slip by crossing controls — normally by applying left rudder and right aileron simultaneously. You can do it the other way, but then

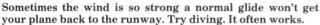

Sometimes the wind is so strong a normal glide won't get your plane back to the runway. Try diving. It often works.

Other pilots can't watch your plane while flying theirs. It's up to you to do whatever is necessary to avoid hitting them — even if that means deliberately crashing your plane.

the sticks get uncomfortably close to each other. In this configuration one control tries to roll the plane left and the other tries to roll it right. You adjust until the two balance each other and the plane flies a straight course toward the runway, but with its nose to one side of the flight path. Remember when you do this that because you have so much drag in a slip, you have to keep the nose lower than normal to maintain flying speed. After all, that's what you're trying to do — glide steeply without gaining speed.

On most sport planes the ailerons are more powerful than the rudder, so you start a slip by simply giving full left rudder. This causes the plane to drop its nose and roll to the left, at which point you apply right aileron to level the wings and establish the slip. Unfortunately, some trainers have strong rudders and weak ailerons, so full right aileron is not enough to balance full left rudder. If your plane is one of these the first time you try to slip it, it will roll left and refuse to be leveled by the ailerons. Don't panic if this happens. Just release both controls, then level the wings with ailerons alone, fly back to altitude, and try again, this time using less rudder.

Practice slipping way up high until you're comfortable with it, but when you've mastered it, you will be able to safely slip almost to ground level. It can be a plane saver when you find yourself too high on a dead stick ap-

proach and too close for one last S-turn.

Practice dead stick landings, complete with S-turns and slips, by cutting the engine to idle in different parts of the sky and trying to glide back to the field and touch down without using the throttle. After a while you'll get good at it and rarely have to add power to save the plane. Of course, when you get a real dead stick, the plane will not glide as far as it will with the engine at idle, but if you've done enough simulated dead sticks, you should have little trouble making the adjustment.

Other types of dead stick landings. Sometimes when the engine quits you can't make it back to land into the wind, and have to come in with a tail wind. Especially if the wind is strong, this will be an exciting landing because you're going to come in hot. If your usual landing speed is 25 mph and you have a 10 mph tail wind, you're going to land at 35 mph, or about 40 percent faster than you're used to. With a 20 mph tail wind you won't believe how hot you'll land, but you'll still have to do it.

With the wind behind it your plane will cover more ground for every foot it drops. This means the glide will be flatter, which in turn means you'll have to set up a lower glide path. If you're coming straight in, you can use the S-turn to kill off excess altitude, but you may have to cut back slightly against the wind to avoid reaching the runway too soon.

Having set up for landing, you're going to have to touch down hot, and if the runway is short, you'll have to do so right away. Remember, a rough landing on the field beats running into the trees at the far end. Remember also that your plane will stall at a high ground speed (the airspeed at stall will be the same as always, of course), so don't try to slow down anywhere near as much as you would on a normal landing. Put those wheels on the ground before the controls get mushy.

All you have to do is set up as you would for a normal landing, but keep the nose a shade lower. Your flare should be only enough to prevent the plane from tripping over its nose gear on touchdown. Use little up elevator and let the plane sink. If it bounces back into the air after touchdown, just be sure not to let the nose get too high, and it will settle down again.

Every so often, the engine will quit, leaving you out of reach of both ends of the runway. If you can just barely make the middle of the field, give it a shot. Your plane will be headed toward the flight line, so make sure you don't run into any other pilots, even if you have to dump the plane. Even dead stick, it has enough energy to cause serious injury.

One of the worst dead stick cases occurs when the engine conks out a second or two after takeoff and there's a fence or a line of trees coming up. You won't make it back to the runway, so don't try. At most fields this is a no-win situation and your task is to minimize damage. If you find yourself in this position, avoid colliding with the fence or the trees, even if that means a high-speed landing on rough ground. Often there's room to turn enough to avoid the obstacles and make a slow landing on rough ground, in which case the damage is usually minor. There is a temptation, though, to turn too sharply to reach some softer landing spot. This can result in a stall in which the plane lands on the tip of the low wing and cartwheels, causing a great deal of damage. Avoid the stall, and if at all possible, keep the wings level through touchdown.

Sometimes your plane can be at high altitude when the engine stops and still not be able to reach the field in a normal glide because it is downwind in a heavy breeze. If you take an ordinary trainer up in a 30 mph wind, turn it into that wind, shut off the engine, and set the plane into a 30 mph glide, it will fly normally except that with respect to the ground, there will be no forward motion and the plane will descend vertically.

One advantage to the vertical glide is that even if the plane lands off field, it will probably not be damaged because its ground speed will be near zero when it lands. The disadvantages are first, that you'll have to walk some distance to retrieve your plane, and second, that since the air near the ground is normally slower than the air above it, the plane will pick up ground speed before landing or else it will stall. In either case it will take a beating.

Obviously, you'd prefer to land on the field, and since the 30 mph glide, which would be fine in calmer air, won't get the job done, you'll have to go faster by dropping the nose into a dive.

Only a few are foolish enough to fly in 30 mph winds, but almost everyone sooner or later braves 15 mph or more. That won't make your plane descend vertically, but it will substantially steepen the angle of descent (not the angle of attack) and decrease your gliding range. If you find yourself in this situation with a dead engine and realize you can't reach the field with a normal glide, try diving. It may extend your range enough to reach the field or it may not, but it's worth a try.

There are a couple of classic dead stick cases that even experienced fliers often botch. The first of these goes as follows: The plane flies parallel to the runway and 50 or 75 yards out. It has a tail wind and is equidistant from both ends of the runway and about 50 feet high when the engine stops.

For some reason, a common response to this event is to continue flying past the end of the runway and then turn into the wind and onto final. Chances are the plane barely has the altitude

The Talon shown here rolled 20 or 30 yards on the runway before flipping over in the weeds. By that time it had slowed enough to avoid damage. Had it hit the runway's end after rolling only a few feet, it probably would have been badly damaged.

and airspeed to complete the turn, let alone glide back to the field against a head wind, and will crash or land short of the runway. If, as sometimes happens, it isn't even able to complete the turn, the outcome will be worse. The plane will stall in the turn, drag one wing on the ground, and cartwheel, tearing itself to pieces.

It doesn't have to be that way. If you get into this situation, either turn immediately or don't turn at all. If you decide you can make the turn, don't hesitate. As soon as the engine quits, roll that plane into as tight a turn as it will hold and bring it into the wind and over the runway. Then level out and set it down. Home free!

Remember that the tail wind will stretch out the first half of the turn, giving you more runway to work with than you would have had if there were no wind and had started at the same place. Even if you end up on the ground and rolling too fast to stop before the runway's all gone, you're probably better off than if the plane hadn't reached the runway at all, because it will have slowed before running into anything.

If you don't have the altitude to complete even this abbreviated turn, just keep flying straight ahead, turning only enough to set down in the flattest place you can find for an off-field landing.

The second classic case is much tougher to handle. The scene is the same except that the plane is going the other way when the motor stops — into the wind this time — and you are faced with having to make a downwind landing after the turn, if you decide to turn. If your runway is 2,000 feet long, and if you have the altitude to turn the plane around, do so immediately and land at your leisure. However, if you're flying from a more typical RC runway of 300 to 500 feet, you probably don't want to make the turn, because even if the plane gets all the way around and you get the wings level, you will have to make a downwind landing, probably on less than half the runway.

Remember, the head wind will flatten the first part of this turn; it will then become a tail wind and stretch the glide.

Most of the time, the better decision is to just fly straight ahead and look for a flat spot where you can set down while flying into the wind. With luck, the damage will be minor. If you turn and don't make it, the consequences will almost certainly be much worse.

Each dead stick landing is unique and will have to be analyzed instantly on its own merits, but if you've studied the examples given here and have practiced them with the engine at idle, you'll be able to get back to the field in one piece almost every time the engine stops.

By the time you can do everything described in this chapter, you'll probably be one of the better fliers in the club. No doubt others will be flashier, but don't be too impressed by their antics in the sky unless they can do them precisely and unless they can land and take off well under any weather conditions short of a tornado. Aerobatics may look spectacular, but a good landing is much tougher than a good vertical roll or loop or spin.

That's not to downplay aerobatic maneuvers. They can be pretty and fun, and if done with precision, are extremely demanding — which is why aerobatics is the subject of the next chapter.

After several seasons of practice, you should feel as comfortable flying inverted as upright, though perhaps not at such low altitudes as here. These planes were designed, built, and flown by Dewey Soltow. Each features a symmetrical airfoil, a necessity on any fully aerobatic plane. Install a large engine on your aerobatic trainer and keep the wing loading light.

10. Aerobatics

Sooner or later, everybody who flies RC learns something about aerobatics, if only by accident. But most of the time, most people just fly around, content with traffic patterns and touch and goes and the occasional loop or roll. Nothing wrong with that, but if you tire of the same old thing, a serious aerobatic maneuver here and there should wake you up. Practicing aerobatics will teach you to fly with precision and you'll learn how to extricate yourself from unexpected situations in ordinary flying. More to the point, it's fun.

Choosing an aerobatic trainer. If you're still flying that trainer with the flat-bottom or semi-symmetrical wing, it's time to move up to a model with a symmetrical airfoil. If your trainer is a modified Box Fly or Great Planes RCM 60, or some other plane with a symmetrical foil, you can use it for aerobatic training. However, you're probably looking forward to a new plane anyway, so you might as well build your first low-wing sport plane. You'll want something with lots of wing, lots of power, and not much weight. A wing loading of about 18 ounces per square foot or a bit less is ideal.

For some reason the commercial pickings have been slim in this department — so slim that when I decided to move to aerobatics, I designed my own Chickenship with 667 square inches of wing area, a weight of less than five

pounds, and a .45 Schnuerle up front. If you know a little about airplane design you can build something like that yourself, but if you don't want to spend time scratchbuilding you will have to settle

Some high-wing trainers such as this RCM 60 fly nicely upside down.

for a kit. The Great Planes Super Sportster and Midwest Pattern Master are among the better offerings. The Diablo, which is an ARF, is also a good choice. Whichever plane you use, be sure to install lots of engine.

At this point you want something that will fly through aerobatic maneuvers slowly, so stay away from the really hot ships. The Sig Kougar and the EZ Talon, for example, are great-flying airplanes, but try something slower until you're sure of yourself. You don't need a surprise as you pull out of a dive inverted.

Once you've built the new plane, ask someone who regularly flies low-wingers to flight test it for you. Low-wing flying isn't especially difficult, but is different. Unlike a high-wing trainer, an aerobatic plane requires you to fly all the time. It does exactly what you tell it to do, no more and no less. If you roll into a 45-degree bank and let go of the stick, it will stay banked and will not try to right itself as your trainer did. In some ways this makes flying easier, but it takes a few flights to get used to. Once you are comfortable with the new plane, practice all the old maneuvers (except the slip) for a while. Then prepare to get uncomfortable again because you are about to fly inverted.

Inverted flight. Most instructors would start you off on something else because learning to fly inverted is difficult. Yet

The Diablo comes almost ready to fly and is a fine aerobatic trainer.

To roll inverted, just apply aileron pressure until the plane is upside down. Then neutralize the ailerons and apply enough down elevator to keep the nose level.

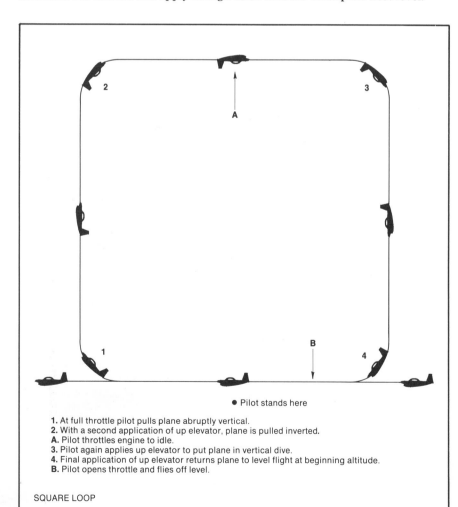

1. At full throttle pilot pulls plane abruptly vertical.
2. With a second application of up elevator, plane is pulled inverted.
A. Pilot throttles engine to idle.
3. Pilot again applies up elevator to put plane in vertical dive.
4. Final application of up elevator returns plane to level flight at beginning altitude.
B. Pilot opens throttle and flies off level.

• Pilot stands here

SQUARE LOOP

it is not nearly so difficult as learning to fly right side up was and it wouldn't be any easier if you first learned how to do a Cuban eight or a roll. Besides you'll have to know how to fly inverted in order to perform more advanced aerobatics and the knowledge may help save your plane if a maneuver goes awry.

There are at least three difficulties with inverted flight for the novice aerobatic pilot.

1. On aerobatic planes, the rudder behaves as if it's working backwards when the plane is upside down. Don't worry about that because you'll rarely use the rudder while flying inverted.

2. The elevator is reversed! Don't ever forget that.

3. If your plane is trimmed to fly hands-off right side up, it will tend to dive when inverted, so you'll be flying an out-of-trim airplane and will have to compensate with down elevator. This takes getting used to. After a few tries, you may want to trim the plane so that it requires some up elevator for level upright flying and an equal amount of down elevator for level inverted flight.

Before starting any aerobatic maneuver, you should have firmly in mind not only what you intend to do and how you intend to do it, but also how you'll get out of trouble if something goes wrong. This is especially true of inverted flight. If anything goes wrong, the safest way to get out of it is to roll the plane upright, providing you have enough airspeed. Nothing difficult about that, but it's not what comes naturally.

When your plane begins to dive on its back, instinct tells you to give up elevator. Fortunately, this works, too, but only if you have plenty of altitude — enough to do a half-loop or split-S, as shown in the illustration. You're probably going to pull out this way more than a few times while you're learning, so be sure you have the altitude to do it.

Also, be sure that once you respond, either by rolling the plane or by split-essing, that you don't change your mind. There is a tendency, after giving full up elevator and seeing the plane unexpectedly dive, to go the other way. Don't do so or you may dig a hole in the ground.

To get started with your first inverted sortie, take the plane to 300 or 400 feet, head into the wind, and half-roll it onto its back. The nose will begin to drop, so use down elevator to bring it back to level flight. Finally, long before the plane gets out of sight, release the down elevator as you roll upright again. You will probably have noticed that it's difficult to force yourself to hold the proper flying attitude with down elevator. This bothers all of us when we start out, but you'll get used to it.

Inverted turns. Practice straight and level inverted flight several more times until you feel comfortable, then start working on inverted turns. They're just like any other turns except for that stupid backwards elevator and the rudder that you'd best not touch.

The ailerons, fortunately, work the same way whether the plane is upside down or not, so use them in the turns as you normally do. Use the elevator, as always, to set the radius of the turn, but when you're flying upside down, you push it down instead of pulling it up. This is nerve-racking for most of us, so we tend to avoid prolonged inverted flying — which is why few RC pilots are really good at it.

During my first season of RC flying I learned the basics, but I hated inverted turns so much I didn't practice enough to get good at them. My second season out, I forced myself to learn by flying two inverted figure eights at the beginning of each flight. Then I would say "Whew!" and relax while I did whatever sort of flying I felt like.

After a few weeks of this, my Little Stik and Chickenship were spending half their time on their backs, often at low altitude, and I was comfortable. The method has a lot to recommend it. As for the fear of learning inverted flight, it's mostly unfounded. I retired the Little Stik after several hundred flights. It's still in the basement somewhere. The Chickenship died a horrible death a couple of years later, not because of all the low inverted flying, but because I tried to land it on a path in the Vermont woods and missed.

Stall turn with half-rolls. Once you have more or less mastered inverted flight, you can turn to other maneuvers. For starters, take that stall turn you learned earlier and put half-rolls in it. To do this, elongate the maneuver to leave room for the half-rolls. Also, remember, after you've done the first half-roll and are about to pivot at the top, to go the other way on the rudder because you're now looking at the underside of the plane. When you get the basic stall turn with half-rolls down pat, you can make an eye-catching maneuver by pulling out inverted instead of upright.

Cuban Eight. Another fairly easy maneuver is the Cuban Eight. Beginning in level flight at about 150 feet, pull up into a loop. The plane will come over the top and start down the other side inverted. As it reaches a 45-degree inverted dive, neutralize the elevator, hesitate briefly, then roll the plane right side up. Continue diving to 150 feet, then pull up into a second loop. Again, when the plane goes over the top and reaches a 45-degree inverted dive, neutralize the elevator, hesitate, roll upright again, and pull out level where you started the maneuver. The loops should be round, the half-rolls should be centered, and both loops should be the same size. It's difficult to fly the maneuver precisely as in

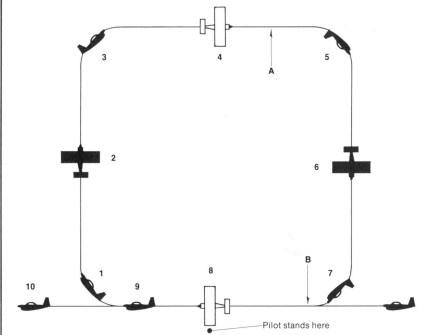

1. With throttle wide open, pilot pulls plane into vertical climb.
2. During the first half of climb pilot applies aileron (right aileron is shown) to begin first half-roll (one quarter-roll below and one quarter-roll above midpoint).
3. Pilot applies down elevator to bring plane level and upright at top of loop, then begins second half-roll.
4. At midpoint of half-roll pilot will see top of plane (note white color in sketch).
A. As plane completes half-roll into inverted flight, pilot reduces throttle to idle.
5. Pilot applies up elevator to put plane into vertical dive, then begins third half-roll.
6. At midpoint of half-roll, pilot will see underside of plane (note dark color).
7. Pilot applies down elevator to pull out inverted at starting altitude.
B. Pilot opens throttle and begins final half-roll.
8. At midpoint of half-roll pilot will see top of plane.
9 and 10. Half-roll completed, plane flies off.

SQUARE LOOP WITH HALF-ROLLS

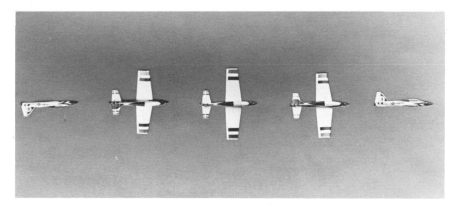

To recover from inverted flight, apply aileron pressure as you neutralize elevator.

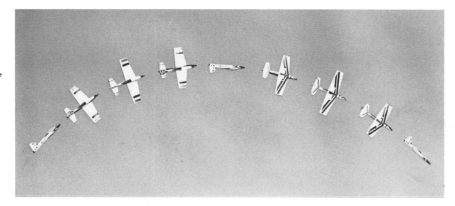

The "humpback" roll is the safest form of roll to practice in the beginning.

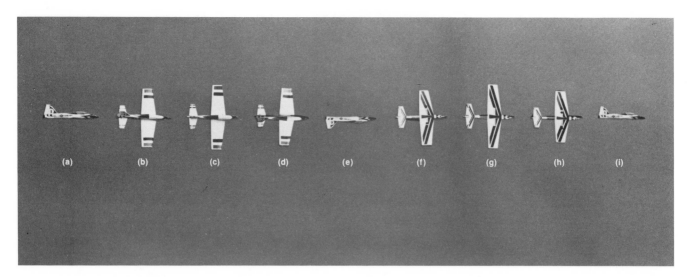

The horizontal roll. (a) Plane in level flight. (b) Pilot rolls plane right. (c) Reaching knife edge. (d) Beginning to apply down elevator. (e) Applying the most down elevator used (not full down). (f) Beginning to release down elevator. (g) Elevator returned to neutral. (h) Beginning to apply up elevator. (i) Returning to level flight.

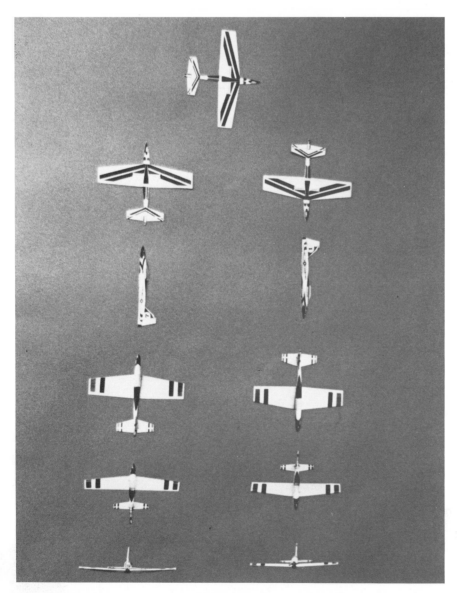

To perform the stall turn with half-rolls, the plane pulls up from level to vertical flight, then does the first half-roll. The pilot cuts the throttle and allows the plane to coast upward. Just before it stops, he applies left rudder (in this example) and a blast of throttle. The plane pivots about its center of gravity and drops straight down. The pilot releases the rudder control, performs a second half-roll, and pulls out at the starting altitude. If this becomes boring, try pulling out inverted.

the drawing, but if your audience is less critical than a contest judge, even a sloppy Cuban Eight looks good.

Horizontal roll. So much for maneuvers where you can look good without being good. The next one is tough — the horizontal roll. Actually, it's not too tough to do one of them, but to put three or more together without wobbling all over the place is a challenge. We'll start with just one roll.

Beginning from level flight, apply full power. When the plane has gained speed, pull the nose up to about 45 degrees, then release the elevator and shove the aileron stick all the way to the right (or left, if you prefer) and watch the plane roll through 360 degrees.

Having completed your first roll, you'll notice that it wasn't very pretty. Blame me for that; I left out part of the instructions and you got a sort of humpbacked roll. The reason for the omission was to give you a feel for the roll without forcing you to remember several new things at once. Next time do it without first pulling into a climb and use down and up elevator alternately to maintain altitude. From level flight, apply full aileron, and as the plane goes inverted, feed in some down elevator. As it comes upright again, use a bit of up elevator. Practice this until you start to get smooth rolls. Then try stringing two and three together.

You won't get everything right in the beginning. One common problem is that the plane loses altitude. If this happens on your rolls, chances are you didn't give enough down elevator while the plane was inverted. If it wobbled all over the place, you probably gave too much of both up and down elevator, or you gave unequal amounts of up and down, or you didn't time the elevator movements properly. Most likely, all these errors were involved at some point.

Unfortunately, there is no perfect

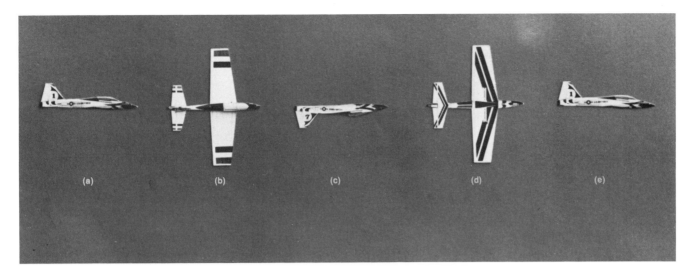

The four-point roll to the right. (a) Level flight. (b) First knife-edge; apply rudder during hesitation. (c) Apply down elevator during hesitation. (d) Apply right rudder during hesitation. (e) Return to level flight. Good-looking four-point rolls require careful coordination of rudder and elevator which comes only after much practice.

roll. No matter what you do, there is going to be some wobble, but you can minimize it to the point that no one will notice if you practice long enough with a given plane. You will find each plane behaves differently and that some are better than others. For example, it is difficult to get smooth rolls with an Ugly Stik, while Hobby Shack's Talon (which you don't need yet) can easily be made to look like it's on a wire.

If you roll to the right, as most people do, your plane will yaw to the left before going inverted, and upon passing through level inverted flight, will begin to yaw right. Similarly, as it approaches upright flight, it will yaw left, then right, as you give up elevator.

The reason for the yawing, of course, is the elevator's rudder-like effect. Remember, this "rudder" turns your plane after you've established a bank, whether you're doing a turn or a roll. It doesn't know the difference. The more elevator movement you give, the more yaw you'll get. The secret is to minimize the amount of elevator required. To do this, move the center of gravity back as far as possible. Be careful when you do this. If you move it too far, you could get an unflyable airplane. Just nudge it back ¼" at a time until the plane gets too sensitive, then move it ¼" forward and settle for that. This makes stall turns more difficult, so you may want to compromise between stall turns and rolls. You can't have everything.

Once you've got the plane properly balanced and trimmed, all you need is practice before you can string three or four rolls together at treetop level. That will take a while. Don't rush it.

Snap roll. Another maneuver you may want to play with is the snap roll. There's nothing much to it. Just fly level at a respectable altitude and apply full elevator, rudder, and aileron simultaneously. The rudder and aile-

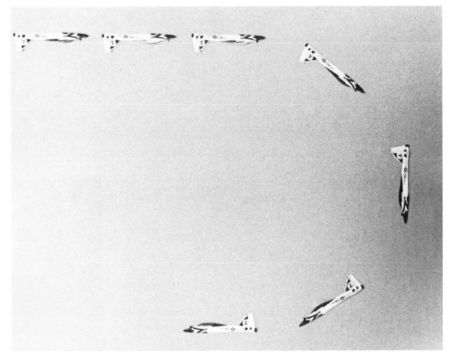

It is also possible to split-ess out of inverted flight by giving up elevator. Be certain you have plenty of altitude and be sure to cut the throttle to idle.

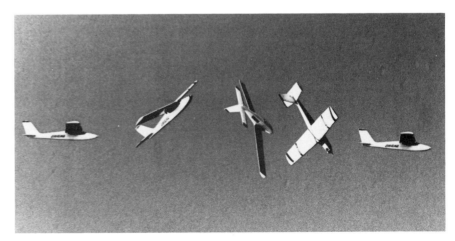

The snap roll. The plane performs a "horizontal spin" and recovers into level flight.

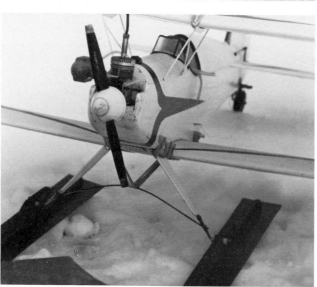

Now you can fly not just trainers, but a wide variety of models such as these. (Clockwise from left) A biplane with home-made skis. The Laser 200, a scale aerobatic model. A quarter scale Stinson Reliant. A home-brew high-performance aerobatic model. (Above) A quarter-scale Piper Cub.

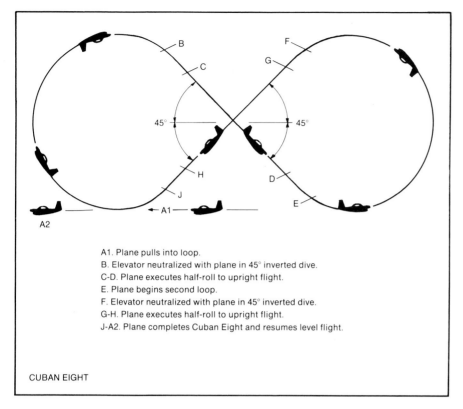

A1. Plane pulls into loop.
B. Elevator neutralized with plane in 45° inverted dive.
C-D. Plane executes half-roll to upright flight.
E. Plane begins second loop.
F. Elevator neutralized with plane in 45° inverted dive.
G-H. Plane executes half-roll to upright flight.
J-A2. Plane completes Cuban Eight and resumes level flight.

CUBAN EIGHT

ron, of course, should be in the same direction. The plane will stall at high speed and perform a sort of horizontal spin. The real skill in performing this maneuver lies in stopping the snap after precisely one turn.

Avalanche. By combining the snap roll with the loop, you can produce another impressive maneuver — the avalanche. To do this, fly into a loop as you normally would. As the plane approaches the top of the loop, give full right (or left) rudder and aileron and full up elevator to make the plane snap. As the snap is completed, release rudder and aileron, chop the throttle, and complete the loop.

Four-point roll. By the time you get this far, you will want to try more sophisticated aerobatic maneuvers. I will describe two of those here: the four-point roll and the square loop with half-rolls. After you've learned those, you'll be on your own.

The four-point roll consists of a single roll with hesitations at 90-degree intervals. It is difficult at first because you have to do several things at once. To start the maneuver, use full power to get the plane moving fast, then roll 90 degrees to the knife-edge position and neutralize the ailerons. As you approach the knife-edge, feed in enough top rudder (left, if you're rolling to the right) to prevent the plane from nosing down.

Hesitate in this position for a second or so, then release the rudder, roll another 90 degrees, feeding in down elevator as the plane rolls inverted.

Hesitate inverted for a second, then release the down elevator and roll an-

other 90 degrees into a second knife-edge and again apply top rudder (this time right rudder if you're rolling right). Hesitate again, then release the rudder and roll 90 degrees to the upright position to complete the maneuver.

In the beginning your four-point rolls will probably be unrecognizable and you'll have to abort more than a few of them, but practice will smooth them out. The tough part is coordinating movements on the sticks. I found it especially difficult to remember to do the second rudder movement in the direction opposite the first. The result was a sudden nose dive in the second knife-edge position. I also forgot to release the down elevator when moving from inverted flight to the second knife-edge. This caused a sharp right turn.

I would analyze what went wrong, then turn around and do it wrong again because by the time I should have released the elevator again, my mind was overloaded trying to remember what to do in the first half of the maneuver. Eventually it all became automatic, as it will for you if you practice enough, and the problem went from making things recognizable to making them pretty. I'm still working on that.

Square loop with half-rolls. One final maneuver to really impress them at the field is the square loop with half-rolls. This is a master's pattern maneuver and is supposed to be too difficult for ordinary mortals. Actually, it's easier than the four-point roll, but scarier.

You learn it in two parts, beginning with the square loop. Line the plane up with the runway, but 50 or 75 yards

out, fly 30 yards or so past where you're standing, and pull up sharply into a vertical climb. This is the first corner. About 60 yards above your starting point, use lots of up elevator to make a second square corner, leaving the plane on its back. Use a little down elevator to keep the nose up, and as the plane flies inverted past where you stand, cut power and coast another 30 yards before you apply up elevator to make the third corner.

Now let the plane dive vertically before applying up elevator again to make the last corner at your starting altitude. Finally, open the throttle and fly the last 60 yards level to complete the maneuver. When you first try the square loop, you should have plenty of altitude, just in case. After you have it down pat, any altitude that lets you feel comfortable on the diving leg will do.

Make sure you're comfortable with the square loop before adding the half-rolls. If you have trouble with the vertical climb, you might consider a more powerful engine or a lighter plane before adding the half-rolls because unless you have good speed on the top leg, it will be difficult to get the maneuver straight and difficult to do the top half-roll.

Now to add the half-rolls: You've already done your share of these in other maneuvers, so there should be no problems there. Remember, though, that when you're inverted, the square corners are done with down elevator, which means you'll give up elevator for the first corner, down elevator for the second, up elevator for the third, and down elevator for the fourth. It's the fourth corner that scares sane people — pulling out inverted from a long vertical dive. I've never seen anyone fail to pull out of an intentional vertical dive, but it does make us all a tad edgy.

I told you it wasn't hard to do. I didn't say it was easy to do well, especially on a windy day. It's tough to make all the legs equal and tougher to get those half-rolls, especially the first and second, straight, so that the whole maneuver will lie in one plane. It's easy to get the first roll a little off and fly out in some odd direction when you make the second corner. Still, even a somewhat lopsided square loop with half-rolls will impress folks at most fields, and if you play around long enough with it, it will start to look pretty good.

If you've mastered everything described up to this point, you can figure out how to do the other maneuvers all by yourself. You certainly don't need me to tell you how. You can also handle a really hot plane now, so before that inevitable time when you bust your aerobatic trainer, start working on something new. Now you can safely fly that Kougar, Talon, Phoenix, or Tiporare or that quarter-scale P-51.

Your first hand launch with the unpowered model should look like this, but you won't need to carry the transmitter.

11. If you have to teach yourself

One of the most exciting (and expensive) things I ever did was teach myself to fly RC. This is not the recommended way to learn. If you decide to do so for the challenge or because you can't find an experienced RC pilot to help you, be aware that even the smallest RC plane can hurt or even kill someone.

If you want to risk your own neck, as I risked mine, that's one thing, but no matter how much the kids beg to come along, don't take them, and don't fly at the local soccer field or school yard, or anywhere there will be other people. It helps to have a buddy along to hand launch your plane, but let him know that he will be exposed to the uncon-

trolled wanderings of a small airplane, that it will be traveling 40 mph or more, and that if it hits him he will first be wounded by a high-speed propeller, then burned by a very hot metal engine.

I make this point not to frighten anyone out of the hobby, but to make sure you know there are risks, especially if you have to fly before you know how. On July 4, 1982, a friend of mine was hit in the chest by an out-of-control RC model and died a few hours later. There are three morals to this story. First, if you have to teach yourself to fly, use the slowest, smallest model you can find. Second, make sure you only en-

danger yourself and other consenting adults. Third, be sure your liability insurance is paid up. That said, let's get on with the subject.

Choosing a trainer. Your first step is to choose a plane. It should be stable, simple, cheap, rugged, easily repairable, and slow. What I have in mind is a small, ready-built foam model that will fly itself if you leave the controls alone. I am aware of only two commercial offerings that fill the bill.

The smallest and the quickest to get into the air is the Cox Centurion. It comes with the engine already installed — all you do is slip the radio gear into precut foam pockets, glue in

You'll need a large field free of obstacles, spectators, and other model aviators.

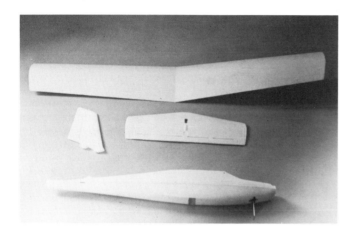

These pieces of foam and a bit of hardware are all there is to a Ranger 42 kit, but when you put them together the model flies respectably on an .049 engine and two controls.

the wing dowels, the stab, and the fin, and put rubber bands in place to hold the wing. The plane can go from the box to the sky in half an hour.

The second plane I recommend, the Goldberg Ranger 42, takes only a few hours of work to prepare for flight. I'd probably pick the Centurion again because it requires less building, but either will do the job and there's not much difference in performance.

When you buy the Centurion, you get the appropriate engine as part of the package. If you choose the Ranger, use a Cox reed-valve .049 engine such as the Babe Bee or Black Widow. Don't use the Cox Tee Dee .049 or .051. These rotary-valve engines have too much power for a beginner to handle and may challenge the structural integrity of the wings as well. To put it in English, if you put a Tee Dee on your plane, the wings may fold when you try to pull out of a dive.

The reed-valve .049 you will use comes with a built-in tank which carries enough fuel for about two minutes

of running time. In the beginning, this will be a long, long two minutes as you struggle to keep the plane up.

Both the Centurion and Ranger can be fitted with more channels than two, but it's hardly worthwhile. The extra weight degrades performance, and in any case, both planes are pretty dull once you know how to fly. Learn the basics on one of these foamies, then move on to a better-flying airplane.

Three equipment notes apply to both the Ranger and Centurion.

1. Both are designed for tricycle landing gear but fly better without it. You should hand launch the model and land on soft ground, so cut off the nose gear and don't bother to install the main gear. Check to be sure the balance point is still correct. If not, fix it before flying.

2. Replace the 450- or 500-mAh battery pack that came with your set. Use a 250-mAh pack. This saves you two ounces, which is a lot on these small models.

3. Reinforce the bottom of the wing

with strapping tape (the kind with fibers in it). Masking tape will not do. Use at least three or four strips of tape extending from one wing tip to the other. To protect the tape from fuel and to add even more strength, cover the wing with a low-temperature heat-shrink material such as Solarfilm. Despite the manufacturer's suggestion, do not paint the model. Paint adds weight you don't need. The finished model should weigh 23 or 24 ounces.

Before attempting to fly, read the instructions that came with your equipment. Then read the rest of this book — especially Chapters 5, 7, 8, and 9. The small engine you will use runs the same as the larger ones except that it has no throttle (engine speed is set before launch by a needle valve) and requires little break-in.

Locating a flying site. Once the airplane is ready and you've educated yourself on its use, you'll have to find a field to fly from. This is not easy in urban areas. Your field should be far from houses and other buildings, and

If the hand-launched plane climbs steeply, stalls, and lands hard, it needs some down elevator trim.

most important, free of people. Since you'll be flying from a hand launch, it needn't be manicured like a golf course (I once flew from an alfalfa field) but it shouldn't have any large obstacles either. If it does (say a tree or two), resign yourself to the fact that unknown powers draw RC planes toward such things. Finally, your field must be large — at least 600 feet on a side — and far from any airport for full-size planes or other RC flying site.

Trimming the model. Let's assume you've found a good field, the plane is ready, and you're eager to fly. Pick a time of day when the wind is nearly calm. Early morning and just before twilight are usually best. Then take your plane out to the field for trimming.

Turn on the transmitter and receiver and set the rudder so it's neutral when the rudder trim tab is neutral. Since your plane has no ailerons, the rudder servo should be connected to the aileron receptacle on the receiver so that the right stick moves the rudder. Set the elevator so it is neutral when the trim tab is neutral. Check to be sure the wing is centered. Measure and mark it; don't trust your unaided eyes. Now remove the prop and prepare for the first test glide.

If possible, arrange to do your test gliding over tall grass because the first

few tries will probably produce rough landings or worse. I will give you a special set of beginner's hand launch instructions for this test. After a bit of practice, you will use a different procedure, but for now, here's how to do it.

With the transmitter and receiver turned on and the transmitter antenna fully extended, check the controls one last time. Then set the transmitter upright on the ground and grasp the plane's fuselage just behind the center of gravity with your throwing hand. If you haven't removed the landing gear, make sure your hand is behind it. Face into the wind. If there is much wind, this is the time to go home. You can't trim your plane in heavy gusts, but you certainly can break it.

If the wind is calm, or at least not more than 5 or 10 mph, all is well and you can do your testing. Even if the wind is light, though, be sure to face into it. In a 5 mph breeze you have to throw the plane 10 mph faster to get flying speed if you face downwind. Hold the plane above your head, run as fast as you can, and heave the airplane, making sure when you let go that the wings are level and the plane is neither climbing or diving. Throw about as hard as if you were casually tossing a ball in the backyard. Don't go for the gold medal javelin throw just yet.

After you've released the model, there is nothing left to do but watch. Be sure to watch closely because what you see will determine how you adjust the plane's trim. There is a tendency to forget exactly what the plane did, which means you'll have to do it over, and that can be rough on your plane.

When you throw it, the model will

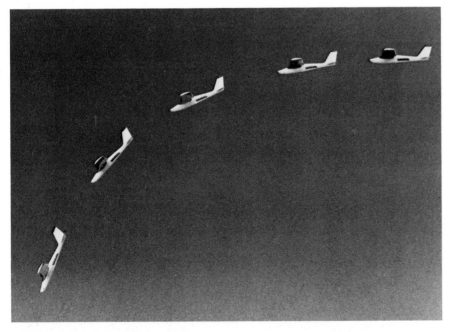

If the plane dives directly into the ground, it needs lots of up elevator trim. First, however, it probably needs repairs — get out the epoxy and toothpicks. The plane shouldn't dive this severely if you set it up correctly and launch it level.

follow one of the following trajectories.

1. Climb, stall, and crash.

2. Dive directly into the ground. This

shouldn't happen if you set the plane up properly.

3. Dive into the ground while rolling left or right.

4. Stall, drop one wing, and dive into the ground.

5. Fly level and land almost gently.

If your plane followed trajectory 5, you are an amazingly lucky person and the model is already trimmed. If you were less lucky, repair any damage with epoxy and toothpicks (toothpicks epoxied into the foam greatly increase the strength of repairs) and make appropriate adjustments before trying again. Be meticulous about getting repaired parts aligned. Even ¹⁄₁₆″ off can cause trouble.

If the plane climbed into a stall, try two or three clicks of down elevator trim. The Rangers I've flown have required an alarming amount of down elevator trim to fly level. Don't let that worry you. Use whatever trim you need. If it dived, use three or four clicks of up elevator trim. If it turned or rolled to the right, use left rudder trim, and if it went left, use right rudder trim. The second flight should be better than the first, but probably not quite perfect. Keep making small adjustments to the trim until you get a smooth flight. The landings will remain a little rough until you can use the transmitter to flare the model just before touchdown. If the glide is good and the plane doesn't hit too hard, you've trimmed it right.

Becoming familiar with the controls. With the trims properly set, you can pick up the transmitter and begin to get a feel for the controls. If you have a helper, let him launch the plane for you. If not, hold the plane in one hand and the transmitter in the other, run hard into the wind, and launch as before. As soon as the plane is released, get both hands on the transmitter (this is the one situation in which you don't use the neck strap). When the plane is only three or four feet up, use up elevator to raise the nose for a flare. If you do it right, the plane should skim the ground a couple of inches up for 10 yards or so before landing gently. The wings will not be perfectly level on ev-

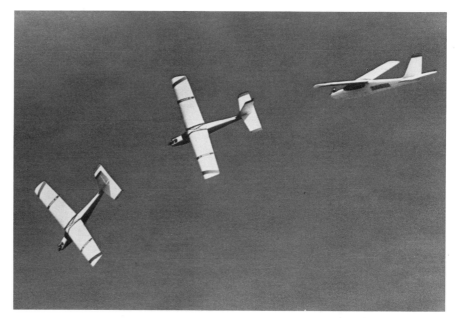

The plane rolls left into a dive and crashes — it's telling you to use right rudder and up elevator trim before the next flight.

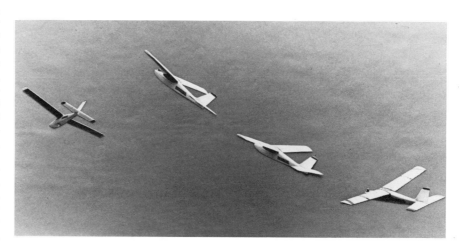

The plane climbs into a stall and drops off on the right wing. It needs down elevator trim and possibly also left rudder trim. Try the elevator first.

ery launch, so try to level them with the rudder as soon as possible. If you can do this, you will greatly improve your landings.

Your next project is to develop more feel for the elevator control. This requires more altitude than you've been getting, so you'll have to learn a new launch technique. Equally important, you will have to fly the plane this time, or it will crash for sure.

Run fast, throw really hard this time, aiming the plane up at an angle of about 15 degrees, and as soon as you can lay hands on the right stick, apply lots of down elevator until the nose be-

The plane is properly trimmed when it flies straight and level without constant control corrections.

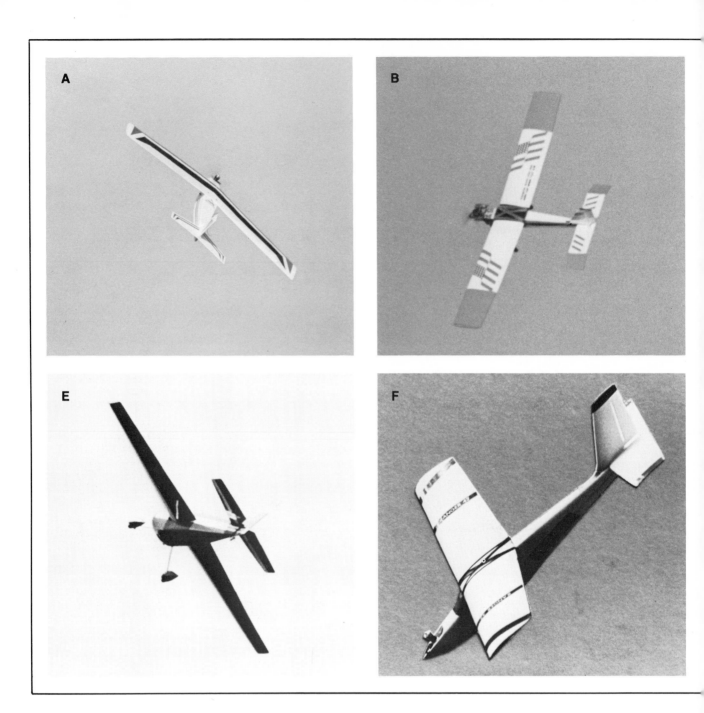

A

B

E

F

gins to drop. If you don't apply it in time, the nose will drop anyway, but by then the wing will be stalled and you will have no way to prevent a crash.

The plane should be about 20 feet up by the time you get the nose down. It will be diving then, and you don't need

that, so ease in enough up elevator to pull the nose back up, not to level flight, but to a good glide angle. Just before it touches down, apply full up elevator to flare for landing. Like everything else in RC, this exercise will take a while to master. Practice until you

can do it consistently and then move on to more creative flying.

Gliding exercises. It's surprising how much you can do with a small model without starting the engine, especially if you have a strong, steady wind. The Ranger shown here has done stall turns and loops from a dead stick hand launch. You won't want to try those maneuvers, but once you get the trim right, here are a number of things you can try to get used to the controls.

First (and this is spectacular in a 20 mph wind), run as fast as you can into the wind, and without breaking stride, fling the plane out at the horizon. This is the time for that gold medal toss. From a standstill, you can probably throw the plane 15 or 20 mph. If you're under 50 and in reasonably good shape, you probably can run 15 mph. If the wind is going 20 mph, the airspeed of

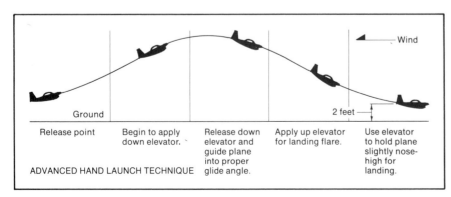

Ground

Wind

2 feet

Release point

Begin to apply down elevator.

Release down elevator and guide plane into proper glide angle.

Apply up elevator for landing flare.

Use elevator to hold plane slightly nose-high for landing.

ADVANCED HAND LAUNCH TECHNIQUE

C

D

The object of these exercises is to look at each photo while holding the transmitter and apply the control pressures required to return the plane to straight and level flight without looking at the answers (cover them with a sheet of paper). Practice until your responses are not only correct, but automatic. It's cheaper to crash pictures than airplanes.

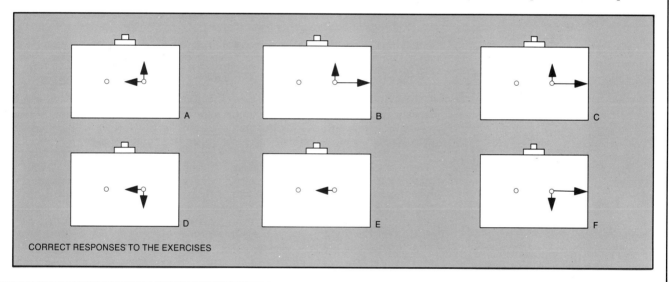

CORRECT RESPONSES TO THE EXERCISES

the plane as it leaves your hand will be roughly 50 mph and it will carry much more kinetic energy than it needs to just fly level. Even if the wind is only 5 or 10 mph, the plane will carry considerable excess energy.

You can use that energy for a number of things, and it will last longer if you convert it to potential energy by climbing. As soon as you release the model, grab for the right transmitter stick and yank it back to force the plane to climb. It will go up like the proverbial shot. In a high wind the plane will climb to 30 or 40 feet if you let it, but use down elevator to set it into a glide at 20 feet or so on the first try.

The first few times you do this, just glide to a landing. (Don't forget to flare just before touchdown.) After you're comfortable with this, try a gentle

turn. The plane will bank and drop its nose. Immediately roll level with the rudder and use the elevator to raise the nose to a reasonable glide angle. When it nears the ground, flare for landing. As you begin to develop a feel for the turns, try to maintain them longer. It is possible without a wind to do a 180-degree turn, and with a strong wind, 360 degrees is not out of the question. Don't rush. Get the feel of this thing.

Once you can manage a 180-degree turn, you'll find the plane headed back toward you. Now rock the wings a little with the rudder. Remember, the rudder will seem reversed and when the plane is coming toward you, you level the wings by moving the right stick to the side of the low wing — the opposite of what you do when the plane flies away from you. Spend a few sessions getting the feel for turns and for handling the

plane when it's headed toward you before going on to powered flight. Play around with it. Become competent and gain confidence. Also, be careful not to hit yourself with the airplane. As slow as it will be going by the time it gets back to you and as light as it is, it probably won't cause serious injury, but at best it will be unpleasant.

Your first powered flights. When you have learned to control your model reasonably well, take it home and prepare for your first powered flight. Charge the batteries the night before your first flight, not the week or month before. On the day of that flight, preflight the airplane (don't forget the range test), fill the fuel tank, turn on the radio system, take the plane to the downwind side of the field, and start your engine.

Launch into the wind, aiming up at

Thrown this way, the Ranger can reach a height of 30 or 40 feet (but don't let it get that high) and travel about 100 yards. This gives you time to feel out the elevator control. If you throw from the top of a hill, you'll have even more time in the air.

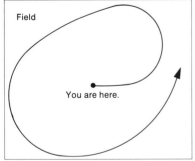

This is the kind of flight path you're shooting for. When the plane is coming toward you, it may help to turn away from it and watch over your shoulder. Whatever you do, don't look away from the plane!

If it's a cloudy day, you may want to fly a circle with yourself at the center. This is easier for the beginner because the plane will never be pointed toward him.

an angle of five or ten degrees. Don't touch the controls at first. Just let the plane climb out on its own if it will. If the nose gets too high or too low, or if a wing drops, you'll have to correct the problem. If you've trimmed the plane properly, it should almost fly itself, making a big left turn. With luck you'll get to 100 feet or so by doing nothing to the controls.

However, since you can't always be lucky, be prepared for the more likely problems. For example, the plane will probably roll into too steep a bank. If that happens, give a little opposite rudder to level the wings — gently. Also, these little foam planes have a tendency for the nose to get too high. This can lead to a stall, so you'll have to get it back down using the elevator as you did earlier in the high-angle launch. Move the controls slowly and deliberately. If you don't panic, you have a chance. If you start over-controlling, your plane will surely crash.

Another likely problem is a plane that can't climb because the engine is too rich or too lean. If you end up short of power and can't make the plane gain altitude, you will have to make a low turn to keep it from either flying out of sight or running into trees or other obstacles. This is not easy even for an expert because even in level flight, the plane is near stall. Your unpowered experience will help a little, but as you begin to turn, it won't hurt to pray. After praying, bring your epoxy to where the plane crashed, repair the damage, then take it back to the launch site and try again — this time with a better needle valve setting.

If you're luckier than this, and the odds are you will be, the plane will climb out nicely on the first try. When it gets to 100 feet or so (about three times the height of a two-story house) apply a little left or right rudder, the direction depending on the layout of your field and the wind direction. The idea is to fly a big circle in front of yourself and upwind, where if you lose control, the wind will carry the model toward you, rather than farther away.

On cloudy days, or when the sun is directly overhead, you can fly the circle from the center, which is easier for the novice. If you try this at other times, there is a good chance the sun will blind you at some point, and after that, you'll have to get out the epoxy and toothpicks and take a long walk.

If the plane banks too steeply as you turn it, neutralize the rudder, and if necessary, go the opposite way until the bank is normal. If the plane is not banked too steeply and is losing altitude, apply up elevator, but not much. If that makes the turn too sharp, release both rudder and elevator. Then apply opposite rudder till the wings are level, followed by enough elevator to bring the plane out of its dive. When the model recovers, try turning again with less bank and less up elevator.

Sooner or later, and the smart money is on sooner, you are going to lose control and have to do two things instantly: Level the wings, and get the plane back to cruising altitude.

Level the wings first because noth-

You'll eventually learn to land smoothly. To keep down weight the plane has no landing gear; it belly-lands just fine.

ing else will work until you do. If the plane is going away from you, just move the rudder the way it feels natural to move it (right stick to the side of the high wing). If the plane is coming toward you, move the stick toward the side of the low wing, no matter how awful it feels to do so. If the plane is in a spiral dive, move the stick in the direction opposite the movement that got you into the spiral. All this happens fast, and your instinct is to over-control, but take it easy. There's usually time to save the plane unless you panic.

Once the wings are level, neutralize the rudder and apply up elevator until the fuselage is level, too. Then try not to do much of anything until you're back to cruising altitude. The idea on your first several flights is not so much to fly the plane as to keep it from crashing. The first two-minute flight will probably be one of the longest periods in your life.

Once the engine stops, the object is not to land neatly on the designated runway, but to get down softly, wherever you can. If you've set the trims properly, you can pretty much ignore the elevator control and concentrate on keeping the wings level and the plane in sight. Don't forget to flare just before touchdown.

Subsequent flights. You're going to make plenty of mistakes at first, and ding your plane more than once, but after a few flights, it will become a better

than even bet that you won't crash. When you have trouble with turns, as all beginners do, re-read the earlier flying chapters and compare what you should be doing with what you are doing. Then go back and practice. It will take a while, but eventually turning will become easy.

Soon you can begin to fly the standard traffic pattern (Chapter 8) rather than just wandering around the sky trying to keep the plane aloft and in sight. By now the two minutes or so your plane stays up will no longer seem like forever. You will begin to fly the plane, rather than follow its lead. Then you can concentrate on flying figure eights and maybe a loop or two to liven up what is (fortunately) becoming a boring few minutes of flight.

When it's time to land, you can also concentrate on gliding back to the field, lining up with the runway, and flaring the plane before touchdown. Don't be upset if you miss the field completely at first or if your landings are awful; just keep at it and soon your flying will become almost smooth. I know about this, having missed the runway on most of my early landing attempts. Eventually the skills come even to the untalented. You may get them sooner.

Trimming a plane in the air. By this time you should be thinking of moving up to a more sophisticated airplane, but before you make that move, learn how to trim a plane in the air because that's what you'll have to do as soon as

you take your new plane up. Your hands will be full then, so learn what you can now.

Launch your plane as before, but once you've gained altitude, push the rudder trim a couple of clicks off its setting and fly the plane briefly this way. Then reset the trim lever so the wings naturally fly level again. Never look down at the transmitter to do this! Next time try the elevator, and finally, both elevator and rudder together. As you gain experience, you can try progressively more drastic out-of-trim settings and combinations until you can handle any flyable trim condition.

From this point on, you should be able to follow pretty much the same program as the fellow with an instructor. You have the advantage that you have already landed the plane. Unfortunately, you haven't yet taken off, which will be the first thing you have to do with your new three-channel trainer. Taking off isn't that tough, though, so re-read the instructions in Chapter 8 and go to it. You will find the three-channel trainer more demanding than your little foam airplane, but at least it won't bore you for a while.

Using a fourth servo for the nosewheel. I've assumed that you already have a new trainer waiting in the wings, and I've called it a "three-channel" plane because it will fly like one. What I had in mind, though, was four channels. Most three-channel planes have the nosewheel steering on the

The Eaglet on the left has ailerons, so needs less dihedral than the other Eaglet that depends on rudder for banking.

This plane took off with too little airspeed. Despite full left aileron, it rolled right and crashed. The pilot should not have tried to take off until he had more airspeed, but if he had used left rudder instead of aileron he just might have made it.

right stick, but virtually all four-channel models have the nosewheel steering on the left stick. In the air you steer a three-channel plane with rudder, rather than ailerons, so you connect the rudder servo to the aileron receptacle in your receiver. But since the nosewheel normally is connected to the same servo as the rudder, it moves to the right stick when the rudder does.

As a result, most people who go through the three-channel phase first learn to steer with the right stick and then have to switch. Since you already have a fourth servo, there's no need to let it go to waste. Install it so that it moves only the nosewheel and make sure that it is operated from the left stick. The only problem with this arrangement is that in some planes there isn't room for a fourth servo inside the fuselage. That's one more argument for a fairly large model.

Put in at least a couple of dozen flights with the plane in the three-channel setup. When you're comfortable flying this way, add ailerons.

Reducing the dihedral. Until this point, you will have needed lots of dihedral in the wing to make the rudder effective. When you add ailerons, too much dihedral will detract from performance, so you will have to cut the wing in half and decrease the dihedral. This is a nuisance, but it's easier than building a new wing, which is the alternative. To make the change, use the procedure in Chapter 3 for correcting misaligned wing panels.

The new plane will fly differently than your old foamie. It will be faster, and with full power, much friskier. But you will be able to slow it down with the throttle when you get into trouble, and when you make a bad landing approach, you can simply open the throttle and go around for another try.

Learning to use the ailerons. A few cautions about ailerons: Set them up for the minimum recommended throw at first. The docility of your model depends more on aileron sensitivity than anything else except balance location.

Second, be constantly aware that if you forget to ease up on the ailerons in a turn, they are much more likely than rudder to roll your plane on its back. Don't let that happen until you're ready to learn inverted flight!

The only other differences you'll notice about ailerons are that when flying at cruising speed your plane rolls more crisply into the turns and that you'll need less up elevator to fly turns.

That's at cruising speed, though. The third caution is that at low speeds, ailerons may become ineffective or even turn the plane the wrong way. Later, when you have more experience, you will learn to cope with this problem by steering with rudder at low speed. For now you'll do well to recognize the problem and solve it by simply increasing airspeed.

Curing a floater. You may find that your new airplane tends to float, that it just doesn't want to settle down and land when you flare it. This may be partly due to a too-fast engine idle, so

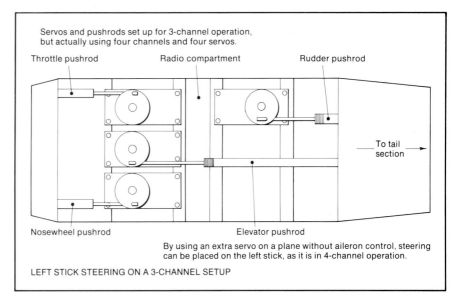

Servos and pushrods set up for 3-channel operation, but actually using four channels and four servos.

Throttle pushrod   Radio compartment   Rudder pushrod

To tail section

Nosewheel pushrod   Elevator pushrod

By using an extra servo on a plane without aileron control, steering can be placed on the left stick, as it is in 4-channel operation.

LEFT STICK STEERING ON A 3-CHANNEL SETUP

before taking off make sure the idle is as low as is compatible with reliable performance.

If you do have a floater, the obvious solution is to lower the engine's idle speed. If you've set the engine up right in the first place, you can do this in the air by just moving the throttle trim lever. Reduce it one click after your first landing attempt. If you then make another pass and the plane still floats, try another click and another landing approach. If you're getting low on fuel and the plane won't give you time for

all these passes, line up on final approach, fly the plane over the runway's end, and use the throttle trim lever to kill the engine. This will get you down in one piece — after which you should adjust that idle.

If you've managed to get your plane to do all the things described in this chapter, congratulations! You've done the nearly impossible and taught yourself to fly by radio.

Now you can concentrate on getting good at it. Chapter 9 should be especially helpful.

Photo credits

Bill Cann, 52, top left. Frank Carroll, 14, top left. John Carroll Sr., 36, large photo. Royal Murray, 9, top left; 57, top right; 74; 80; 81. Chuck Porter, 51, top right; 78, lower left. Dewey Soltow, 75, top. Bonnie Tyrrell, 30, top right; 31, lower. All other photographs by John Carroll.

Useful addresses

Academy of Model Aeronautics
1810 Samuel Morse Drive
Reston, VA 22090

Ace R/C, Inc.
Box 511, 116 West 19th Street
Higginsville, MO 64037

Aero Composites
411 Townsend Place
Dayton, OH 45431

Airtronics Inc.
11 Autry
Irvine, CA 92718

Circus Hobbies, Inc.
3132 South Highland Drive
Las Vegas, NV 89109

Cox Hobbies, Inc.
1525 East Warner Avenue
Santa Ana, CA 92705

Craft Air
20115 Nordhoff Street
Chatsworth, CA 91311

Fox Manufacturing Co.
5305 Towson Avenue
Fort Smith, AR 72901

Futaba Corporation of America
4 Studebaker
Irvine, CA 92718

Carl Goldberg Models, Inc.
4734 West Chicago Avenue
Chicago, IL 60651

**Great Planes Model
Manufacturing Company**
PO Box 4021
Champaign, IL 61824-4021

Hobbypoxy Products
39 Pine Street
Rockaway, NJ 07866

Hobby Shack
18480 Bandilier Circle
Fountain Valley, CA 92728-8610

McDaniel R/C
1654 Crofton Blvd., Suite #4
Crofton, MD 21114

Midwest Products Co., Inc.
400 South Indiana Street
Hobart, IN 46342

**Pacer Technology
and Resources**
9420 Santa Anita Ave.
Rancho Cucamongo, CA 91730

**Pactra Industries,
Hobby Division**
16946 Sherman Way
Van Nuys, CA 91406

Rocket City Specialties
103 Wholesale Avenue
Huntsville, AL 35811

Sig Manufacturing Co., Inc.
401 South Front Street
Montezuma, IA 50171

Tower Hobbies
P. O. Box 778
Champaign, IL 61820

Windsor Propeller Company
3219 Monier Circle
Rancho Cordova, CA 95742

Wing Manufacturing Co.
306 East Simmons Street
Galesburg, IL 61401

World Engines, Inc.
8960 Rossash Avenue
Cincinnati, OH 45236

Acknowledgments

There may be only one name on the cover, but this book could not have been written without help from many quarters. I would like to thank all the members of the Northern Virginia Radio Control club who put up with me and my camera for a whole year and posed their models in the air and on the ground. Special thanks go to Brad Baylor, Bill Cann Sr., Bob Chatman, Frank Himmerich, Fred and Shawn Locks, Dave Humphreys, Luther Hux, Bill Hershberger, Doug Pratt, Dick Roe, Larry Parfitt, Charles Porter, Dewey Soltow, and Steve Tyrell, all of whom at one time or another flew their models for the camera. Thanks also for technical help from many of those pilots and from Larry Hutson and Bernie Stuecker.

Hobby Shack provided Box Fly and Talon kits, Carl Goldberg Models supplied an Eaglet kit, and Fox Manufacturing Co. donated the superb Fox .19 used to power the Eaglet. World Engines, Tower Hobbies, Ace R/C, Circus Hobbies, Cox Hobbies, and Airtronics provided valuable information, and Bill and John Huson of Model Masters were helpful throughout the project.

Finally, my thanks to the woman in my life, who says she'll leave if I put her name in the book. She has been patient and supportive through this and other time-consuming projects.